D0659929

The Reformed Handbook

About "Winking Calvin"

The wink on John Calvin's face indicates that even though theology is serious stuff, we should nonetheless remember that it is not our theology that saves us, but Jesus Christ. Therefore, our life in the church can be buoyant, and our theological wranglings can be done with a sense of humor and love for our neighbor.

The Reformed Handbook

Faith Alive Christian Resources
Grand Rapids, Michigan

THE REFORMED HANDBOOK

Part of this book was originally published as The Lutheran Handbook, © 2005 Augsburg Fortress.

Elements of Worst-Case Scenario Survival Handbook ® trade dress have been used with permission of and under license from Quirk Productions, Inc. Based on the trade dress of The Worst-Case Scenario Survival Handbook Series by Joshua Piven and David Borgenicht, published by Chronicle Books, LLC, Worst-Case Scenario ® and the Worst-Case Scenario Survival Handbook ® are registered trademarks of Quirk Productions, Inc., 215 Church Street, Philadelphia, PA 19106.

Scripture quotations are from the New Revised Standard Version Bible, © 1989, Division of Christian Education of the National Council of the Churches of Christ in the United States of America.

Pages 67-75: Sources for the charts include reference materials from *Information Please*, New York Times Public Library/Hyperion, Rose Publishing, Statistics Canada, Time-Life, and Wadsworth Group/Thomas Learning.

Page 84: Sources for "Calvin's Words in a Motto and Seal" includes an essay by Barbara Carvill, "Minds and Hearts in the Making."

Page130: Source for "Some of John Calvin's Key Thoughts on Spiritual Living" includes "Reformed Thought on Prayer and the Spiritual Life" prepared by Steve Shussett.

Page 130: Source for "Some of John Calvin's Key Thoughts on Spiritual Living": *Institutes of the Christian Religion* by John Calvin, ed. John T. McNeill; tr. Ford Lewis Battles. The Library of Christian Classics, © 1960 The Westminster Press.

Pages 200-221: Excerpts from the Heidelberg Catechism © 1975, 1988 Faith Alive Christian Resources.

Cover design: Pete Euwema

Cover illustration: Scott Holladay

Interior illustrations: Brenda Brown and April Hartmann

Contributing writers: Suzanne Burke, Lou Carlozo, Giacomo Cassese, James Dekker, Mark Gardner, Wes Halula, Sarah Henrich, Mark Hinton, Sue Houglum, Rolf Jacobson, Susan M. Lang, Andrea Lee, Daniel Levitin, Terry Marks, Catherine Malotky, Jeffrey S. Nelson, Rebecca Ninke, Eliseo Pérez-Alvarez, Dawn Rundman, Jonathan Rundman, Tod Schroeder, Ken Sundet Jones, Hans Wiersma

ISBN 978-1-59255-297-9

10 9 8 7 6 5 4 3 2 1

CONTENTS

This Book Belongs To	10
About My Congregation	11
Preface	12

Church Stuff

15

How to Get to Know Your Pastor	16
How to Survive for One Hour in an Un-Air-Conditioned Church	18
How to Survive for an Hour in a Church with a Faulty Furnace	20
How to Respond When Someone Sits in "Your Place"	21
How to Use a Worship Bulletin	23
How to Sing a Hymn	26
How to Sing a Praise Song	29
How to Listen to a Sermon	31
How to Respond to a Disruption During Worship	33
The Anatomy of a Baptism	36
How to Receive Communion	38
How to Pass the Offering Plate	43
How to Pass the Peace in Church	46
How to Stay Alert in Church	48
What to Bring to a Church Potluck (by Region)	50
Important Things the Reformers Wrote and Why They're Still Important Today	54
Five Things You Should Know About the Reformation	57

Five Facts about Life in Medieval Times   59

History's Seven Most Notorious Heretics   61

How to Avoid Getting Burned at the Stake   64

Charts and Diagrams

• World Religions   67

• Comparative Religions   68

• Family Tree of Christianity   70

• U.S. and Canadian Christian Denominations   71

• Comparative Denominations   72

• The Seasons of the Church Year and What They Mean   76

• The Seasons of the Church Year (diagram)   80

• Martin Luther (portrait)   82

• John Calvin (portrait)   83

• Calvin's Words in a Motto and Seal   84

Everyday Stuff   87

John Calvin's "Three Uses of God's Law"   88

How to Share Your Faith with Someone   89

How to Pray   92

How to Work for Peace and Justice on Behalf of People
    Who Are Poor and Oppressed   95

How to Identify a Genuine Miracle   98

Three Essential Personal Spiritual Practices   100

How to Forgive Someone   104

How to Confess Your Sins and Receive Forgiveness   106

How to Defend Your Faith Against Attack   108

How to Resist Temptation   111

How to Care for the Sick   114

How to Identify and Avoid Evil   116

How to Avoid Gossip   118

How to Resolve Interpersonal Conflict   120

How to Comfort Someone   123

How to Cope with Loss and Grief   124

The Top Ten Attributes to Look for in a Spouse   127

Some of John Calvin's Key Thoughts on Spiritual Living   130

How to Distinguish Between a Job and a Calling   132

How to Be Saved (by Grace Through Faith and
    Not by Good Works)   134

How to Reform the Church When It Strays from the Gospel   137

How to Tell a Sinner from a Saint (diagram)   139

How to Understand the Trinity as One God in Three Persons 140

Bible Stuff   143

Common English Translations of the Bible   144

Sixty Essential Bible Stories   146

How to Read the Bible   149

How to Memorize a Bible Verse   151

The Top Ten Bible Villains   154

The Top Ten Bible Heroes   157

The Three Most Rebellious Things Jesus Did   160

The Seven Funniest Bible Stories   161

The Five Grossest Bible Stories   164

Five Facts about Life in Old Testament Times   166

Ten Important Things that Happened
    between the Old and New Testaments   167

Five Facts about Life in New Testament Times   170

The Five Biggest Misconceptions about the Bible   172

Jesus' Twelve Apostles (Plus Judas and Paul)   175

The Five Weirdest Laws in the Old Testament   177

The Top Ten Bible Miracles and What They Mean   179

Maps and Diagrams

• The Exodus   181

• The Holy Land—Old Testament Times   182

• The Holy Land—New Testament Times   183

• Paul's Journeys   184

• Jerusalem in Jesus' Time   186

• Noah's Ark   187

• The Ark of the Covenant   188

• Solomon's Temple   189

• The Armor of God   190

• The Passion and Crucifixion   191

The Heidelberg Catechism

Introduction   200

Part I: Misery (Q&A 3-11)   202

Part II: Deliverance (Q&A 12-85)   203

The Apostles' Creed   204

The Trinity   205

The Sacraments   213

Part III: Gratitude   218

The Ten Commandments   219

The Lord's Prayer   221

Notes & Stuff   222

This Book Belongs To

Name _____

Address _____

_____

E-mail _____

Telephone _____

Birth date _____

Baptism date _____

Date of public profession of faith _____

Parents' names

_____

_____

_____

_____

_____

Churches I've belonged to: *Years of membership*

_____   _____

_____   _____

_____   _____

_____   _____

_____   _____

_____   _____

About My Congregation

Name _____

Address _____

_____

Year organized/founded _____

My pastor(s) _____

_____

_____

_____

Number of members _____

Average weekly worship attendance _____

Facts about my denomination _____

_____

_____

_____

Other information about my congregation and faith

_____

_____

_____

_____

✠

PREFACE

Please Be Advised:

Many books, pamphlets, and booklets have been written
through the centuries as companions for ordinary people
who wanted help navigating their way through a complicated subject. Even in the age of Google real paper and print
books are helpful resources for learning the basics of a given
subject or for handy review. *The Boy Scout Handbook* comes to
mind, for example. So do *The American Red Cross First Aid and
Safety Handbook, Tune and Repair Your Own Piano: A Practical
and Theoretical Guide to the Tuning of All Keyboard Stringed
Instruments,* and *National Audubon Society's Field Guide to
North American Reptiles and Amphibians.* They stand as testimony to the ordinary person's need for a guide to both the
vast truths and complex detail that make up a particular area
of interest. These books turn complicated, inaccessible ideas
into simple, easy-to-understand concepts, and, if necessary,
into action steps that are easy to follow.

The Reformed Handbook follows the format of many hand-
books. Here, you will discover a combination of reliable,
historical, and theological information alongside some fun
facts and very practical tips on being a churchgoing follower
of Jesus Christ. Because we consider anyone who purchases
or receives this handbook to be a discerning reader, we have
occasionally added some outrageously fictitious items that
test your skills of sifting fact from fiction, thus raising the IQ
of English-reading Reformed people.

You will also discover that this book is intended for learning
and enjoyment. (Some Reformed people have trouble doing
the latter until they've first suffered through the former.)

It's meant to spur conversation, to inform and edify, and to make you laugh. Think of the book as a comedian with a dry sense of humor and a degree in theology (with about a B-average). It can be used in the classroom with students or at the dinner table with family or in solitude.

But however you use it, use it! We've cut the corners off so you can throw it in your backpack or stuff it in a pocket. It's printed on paper that accepts either ink or pencil nicely, so feel free to write and highlight in it (and there's room for notes in the back). The cover is this fancy, nearly indestructible stuff that will last nearly forever too, so don't worry about spilling soft drinks or coffee on it. We've even heard it can sustain a direct hit from a Play Station Three! (But don't expect it to protect you from a bullet through the heart like the proverbial New Testament of soldiers the world over.)

Anyway, the point is this: Being a follower of Jesus is hard enough without having to navigate the faith journey—let alone the maze of church culture—all alone. Sooner or later everyone needs a companion.

—THE EDITORS

CHURCH STUFF

Every well-prepared Reformed person should have a basic understanding of Reformed teachings and where they came from.

Plus, since every congregation goes about worship in a slightly different way, it might take a little time to get the hang of things—especially if you're new to a congregation.

This section includes:

- Essential facts about the Reformed expression of the Christian faith. (If you know these things, you'll know more than most—but don't boast about anything except grandchildren and that you belong to Jesus Christ.)

- Practical advice for singing hymns, taking communion, and getting to know the people in your congregation.

- Hints for enjoying worship—even when you're having a bad day.

HOW TO GET TO KNOW YOUR PASTOR

Pastors play an important role in the daily life of your congregation and the community. Even though they know Greek and Hebrew—well, almost all of them *learned it once*, though they may have forgotten—pastors experience the same kinds of ups and downs as everyone else. They value your efforts to meet, connect with, and support them.

❶ **Connect with your pastor after worship.**
After the worship service, join others in line to shake the pastor's hand. Sharing a comment about the sermon, readings, or hymns lets the pastor know that his or her worship planning time is appreciated. If your congregation doesn't shake hands with the pastor on the way out of the worship space, find other ways to make that personal connection.

❷ **Pray daily for your pastor, because he or she doesn't just work on Sunday.**
Your pastor has many responsibilities, like visiting members in the hospital, writing sermons, and figuring out who can help drain the flooded church basement. In your prayers, ask God to grant your pastor health, strength, and wisdom to face the many challenges of leading a congregation.

❸ **Ask your pastor to share with you why he or she entered ordained ministry.**
There are many reasons why a pastor may have enrolled in seminary to become an ordained minister. Be prepared for a story that may surprise you.

❹ **Stop by your pastor's office to talk, or consider making an appointment to get to know him or her.**
Pastors welcome the opportunity to connect with church members at times other than worship. As you would with any drop-in visit, be sensitive to the fact that your pastor

may be quite busy. But sometimes the pastor is just waiting for a "blessed interruption"—perhaps on a Thursday afternoon after two frustrating days of working on Sunday's sermon, which is simply not behaving itself. A break with a real person who wants to chat for 10 or 15 minutes often does something unexpected to freshen the pastor's spirit and mind. Afterward, insights come, sentences flow, and God's Word comes alive for the pastor and, three days later, for the congregation.

Getting to know your pastor can
help you to get more out of church.

HOW TO SURVIVE FOR ONE HOUR IN AN UN-AIR-CONDITIONED CHURCH

Getting trapped in an overheated sanctuary is a common churchgoing experience. The key is to minimize your heat gain and electrolyte loss.

❶ Plan ahead.
When possible, scout out the sanctuary ahead of time to locate optimal seating near fans or open windows. Consider where the sun will be during the worship service and avoid sitting under direct sunlight. Bring a bottle of water for each person in your group.

❷ Maintain your distance from others.
Human beings disperse heat and moisture as a means of cooling themselves. An average-size person puts off about as much heat as a 75-watt lightbulb. The front row will likely be empty and available. Think of it as a box seat at the most important game in town! Your pastor will notice if you sit there.

Use your bulletin as a personal fan to keep cool.

❸ Remain still.
Fidgeting will only make you hotter and sweatier. You may wish to assume a comfortable posture of sitting slightly forward and clasping your hands.

❹ Think cool thoughts.
Your mental state can affect your physical disposition. If the heat distracts you from worship, imagine you're sitting on a big block of ice.

❺ Dress for survival.
Wear only cool, breathable fabrics.

❻ Pray.
Jesus survived on prayer in the desert for forty days. Lifting and extending your arms in an open prayer position may help cool your body by dispersing excess heat. If you've been perspiring, though, avoid exposing others to your personal odor. Be sure to use deodorant.

Be Aware

- Carry a personal fan—or use your bulletin as a substitute.

- Worship services scheduled for one hour sometimes will run longer, especially if there are baptisms, Lord's Supper, or commissioning of mission teams. Plan ahead.

HOW TO SURVIVE FOR AN HOUR IN A CHURCH WITH A FAULTY FURNACE

❶ Go with the layered look
North of the 49th parallel this may require wearing long johns (preferably wooly and itchy), polar fleece with a full zipper (in case the furnace goes on), mittens with flip-off finger covers so you can turn the pages in the hymnbook and Bible, a toque and Nipigon Nylons *(if you have to look these words up, you aren't going to church where you need them, so don't worry)* and breathable windproof shell and pants.

❷ Sit as close to your significant other as parents or said other will permit.
It is OK to hold hands during the sermon, but be sure to allow sufficient space to get into your purse, wallet, or pocket to find money for the offering.

❸ Sing with enthusiasm—it warms you up.

❹ Sit as far away from the drafty windows and leaky doors as possible.

HOW TO RESPOND WHEN SOMEONE SITS IN "YOUR PLACE"

Even though you or your family may have sat in that pew for eighty-six years, realize that *it's not your pew.* A worship service is a public event intended to welcome people into God's presence; thus God's people should welcome visitors—not wave and squawk like a wounded gull because someone else took "your spot." If you make a big deal about someone sitting in your spot, you will probably push that person away.

❶ **Recognize personal space.**
   We all carry a bubble of personal space, which differs from culture to culture. For North Americans and Europeans, it's about a foot and a half. For many Latin Americans, it's about half that. Wherever on the spectrum you happen to fall, there are certain situations in which we invite visitors into our little sphere of experience—like at church. Furthermore, human beings are territorial in nature and sometimes see strangers inside the bubble as an affront. These situations need not be cause for alarm.

❷ **Smile and greet the "intruders."**
   These folks aren't intruders—they're guests, visitors to your congregation, new blood. Avoid creating bad blood you might regret later on. Make solid eye contact so they know you mean it, shake hands with them, and leave no impression that they've done something wrong by sitting where you usually sit.

❸ **View the "intrusion" as an opportunity.**
   Remember, you don't own the pew; you just borrow it once (or twice) a week. Take the opportunity to get out of

your rut and sit someplace new. This will physically emphasize a change in your perspective and may yield new spiritual discoveries.

❹ If you can tell that your new friends feel uncomfortable at having displaced you, despite your efforts to the contrary, make an extra effort to welcome them.

Consider inviting them for coffee or lunch after worship to become acquainted. If you go to a restaurant and there are too many people for you to foot the bill, consider inviting them to accompany you on a "go Dutch" basis. This will eliminate any hierarchy and place you on equal footing.

HOW TO USE A
WORSHIP BULLETIN

Most Reformed congregations offer a printed bulletin to assist worshipers. Many use a projection and screen system to help you navigate through the service. Bulletins and overheads usually show the order of the service, the sections of the worship service, music listings, the day's Bible readings, prayers, and important community announcements.

❶ Arrive early.
A few extra minutes before worship will allow you to scan the bulletin and prepare for the service.

❷ Receive the bulletin from the usher.
Upon entering the worship space, an usher will give you a bulletin. Some congregations stack bulletins near the entrance for self-service.

❸ Review the order of worship.
When seated, open the bulletin and find the order of the service, usually printed on the first or second page or inserted in a contrasting color. Some churches print the entire service in the bulletin so worshipers don't have to switch back and forth between worship aids.

❹ Determine whether other worship resources are required.
The order of worship may specify additional hymnals, song sheets, candles, or other external supplies required during the service.

❺ Fill out the attendance or welcome card.
A card may be located inside the bulletin or somewhere in your row. Fill it out completely. You may be asked to pass this card to an usher or to place it in the offering plate or bag. Some congregations have visitors' books for people to sign.

⑥ Reflect on bulletin artwork.
Bulletin covers or visuals on the projection screen often feature a drawing or design that corresponds to the season of the church year or the day's Bible verses. In some congregations children's artwork is used for bulletin covers related to specific themes in worship. Look carefully at the artwork and make a note of its connection to the lessons or sermon.

⑦ Track your worship progress.
The bulletin or projection screen will guide you through the order of worship (called "liturgy" in many churches), hymns, Bible readings, and prayers as you worship. This will let you know where you are at all times and help you get back to where you should be if you nod off during a dull hymn or confusing bits in the pastor's message.

⑧ Watch for responsive readings.
Worship is a conversation between God and believers and among believers themselves. So the bulletin and/or screen may include spoken responsive readings in which the congregation participates. The worship leader's parts may be marked "Pastor" or "Leader." The congregation's responses may be marked "People" and are often printed in **boldface type**.

⑨ Find and follow the forms for special events such as baptism and communion.
Special events such as baptisms, communion, and professions of faith are usually introduced with readings that have long been part of the tradition. These forms may be found in the back of the songbook or perhaps projected on a screen. Read them. They can teach you a great deal about Reformed worship and history. You probably won't understand everything, but ask long-time members to help you. Maybe they won't know either, but most of them will be glad you asked and will help you answer your question.

⑩ Identify the worship leaders and assistants.
The names of ushers, musicians, greeters, readers, and pastors are often found in the bulletin. Greet these people by name following the service, giving a word of appreciation for their contribution to the worship.

⑪ Review the printed announcements.
Community activities, calendars, and updates are often listed in the back of the bulletin. Scan listings during the prelude music, the offering, or the spoken announcements.

⑫ Make good use of the bulletin after the service.
Some congregations re-use bulletins for later services. Return the bulletin if possible. Recycling bins may also be provided. If you wish, you may take the bulletin home with you. Some churches print a brief outline of the pastor's message, which is helpful for taking notes and paying attention.

Be Aware
- All congregations stand at certain times during worship, especially during singing. The bulletin may use an asterisk in the order of worship to indicate when to stand. Standing

If you choose not to save your worship bulletin, be sure to recycle it whenever possible.

and sitting—even occasional kneeling—aren't for exercise. Rather, they're an important physical participation in worship that helps you focus on the meaning behind the action.

HOW TO SING A HYMN

Music is an important part of the Reformed tradition, a wonderful way to worship God, and an enjoyable way to build community. Hymn singing can be done without demonstrable emotion, but many otherwise stoic Reformed people appropriately channel emotion into their hymn singing and are therefore loud.

There will always be people who make a joyful noise to the Lord in keys nowhere near the one in which the song was written. Try not to laugh. If you must laugh, cover your face with a handkerchief and pretend to sneeze. If you're laughing so hard that tears are falling down your cheeks, your neighbors may think you're powerfully moved by the song!

❶ **Locate hymns in advance.**
As you prepare for worship, consult the worship bulletin or the hymn board to find numbers for the day's hymns. Bookmark these pages in the hymnal using an offering envelope or attendance card. Even if your congregation uses overhead projection for songs and readings, take some time to look through the songbooks if they are in the racks in front of you.

❷ **Familiarize yourself with the hymns.**
Examine the composer credits, the years the composer(s) lived, and whether the tune has a different name than the hymn itself. Notice under what worship heading the song falls: Is it for the beginning of worship? Advent? Christmas? Lent? Easter? Ascension Day? Pentecost? Are the words taken from the Bible? Is this a hymn for a sad or joyful time? Is it a prayer or a celebration? Look in the back of the songbook to find indices for topics, themes, and Bible passages.

❸ **Assist nearby visitors or children.**
Using a hymnal can be confusing. If your neighbors seem disoriented, help them find the correct pages, or let them read from your book.

Support the hymnal's spine with one hand. Place the other on the open page.

❹ **Adopt a posture for best vocal participation.**
Hold the hymnal away from your body at chest level. Place one hand under the spine of the binding, leaving the other hand free to turn the pages. Keep your chin up so you can breathe deeply and your voice projects outward.

❺ **Begin singing.**
If the hymn is unfamiliar, sing the melody for the first stanza. If you read music, explore the written harmony parts during the remaining stanzas. Some neighbors may or may not be in tune; in this event, please see the second paragraph of page 26—and remember: you're not perfect either.

❻ **Focus on the hymn's content.**
Some of the lyrics may connect with a Scripture reading of the day. Certain ones may be especially inspiring.

❼ **Avoid dreariness.**
Hymns are often sung in such a serious way that the congregation forgets to enjoy the music. Sing with energy and feeling appropriate to the hymn. Many hymns show a progression from lament or confession to joy or praise. For example, look up the lovely, haunting versified Psalm 30 rendered as, "I Worship You, O Lord."

Be Aware

- Hymnals are not just for use at church. Consider keeping a personal copy of your congregation's hymnal at home for reference and study. Hymnals also make excellent gifts for baptisms or professions of faith.

- Some hymns use words and phrases that are difficult to understand (such as, "the Father's promised Paraclete" from the hymn "Creator Spirit, by Whose Aid"). Use a dictionary or a Bible with a concordance to clear up any uncertainty.

HOW TO SING A PRAISE SONG

Many Reformed congregations use modern worship styles, often called Praise & Worship (P&W), featuring guitars and drums. In these settings the words are typically displayed on large multimedia projection screens.

❶ Follow the instructions of the song leader.
Someone in the praise band or worship team will invite the congregation to stand up, sit down, repeat certain sections, or divide into men's and women's vocal parts. Pay attention to this person to avoid losing track.

❷ Learn the melody and song structure.
Pay special attention to the melody line sung by the band's lead vocalist. P&W songs can be tricky because they are rarely printed with notated sheet music and are sung differently from place to place.

❸ Sing along with gusto.
Once the melody has been introduced, join in the singing. When you're comfortable with the song, experiment with harmony parts.

❹ Avoid "zoning out."
Singing often-repeated lyrics that are projected on giant screens can result in certain mental numbness. Avoid this by surveying the worship area. Notice banners, liturgical symbols, pulpit, communion table, baptismal font, cross, designs or Bible stories pictured in stained glass windows (especially in older buildings). Make eye contact with other people.

❺ Identify themes in the songs.
Determine whether the song is being used as a confession,

a prayer, a hymn of praise, or whether it serves another purpose. See if you can identify the Bible passages referred to by certain phrases or key references in the hymns.

❻ Watch out for raised hands.
A few Reformed people have learned some very good things from Pentecostal and African-American churches. They may suddenly raise their hands in praise to God during a stirring song. Be sure to give these worshipers plenty of room to avoid losing your glasses or getting a black eye. You might even experience God's presence so powerfully yourself that your own arms fly up without warning!

Be aware of especially passionate worshipers who might raise their hands too quickly.

Be Aware

- Worship is highly participatory. The praise band or worship team is there to help you and the congregation sing and participate in worship, not to perform a concert.
- There are no prohibitions in the Reformed tradition against physical expression during worship.
- In some congregations, certain gestures will draw amused stares, but don't worry about that. God is our main observer when we worship. We know God loves music and praise (see Psalm 150) and was even pleased when David, clothed only in his skivvies, danced his way into Jerusalem in front of the Ark of the Covenant (2 Samuel 6:14, 15). So a little jig during a lively song might be exactly the right response.

HOW TO LISTEN TO A SERMON

Reformed people believe God's Word comes to us through the reading and preaching of Holy Scripture. Honoring God's Word, not to mention getting something out of church, includes diligent listening to the sermon and active mental participation.

❶ Review active listening skills.
While the listener in this case usually doesn't get to speak, the sermon is still a conversation. Make mental notes as you listen. You may experience a variety of emotions—joy or anger or sadness—while listening to the sermon. Don't be surprised if tears pop into your eyes. Notice where and why you react and which emotions you experience.

❷ Take notes.
Note-taking promotes active listening and provides a good basis for later reflection. It also allows you to return to confusing or complicated parts at your own leisure. Some congregations provide space in the bulletin for notes. You may want to take notes and file them according to the Scripture passage on which the sermon is based.

Take notes to recall more information and get more out of the sermon.

❸ Maintain good posture. Avoid slouching.
Sit upright with your feet planted firmly on the ground and your palms on your thighs. Beware of the impulse to slouch or cross your arms as these can encourage drowsiness. Don't lean against your neighbor—whether that is a parent, sibling, or friend—unless that person gives you permission

❹ Listen for the law.
You may feel an emotional pinch when the preacher names the sinner in you. Pay attention to your reaction, and try to focus on waiting for the gospel rather than becoming defensive. For help in understanding and personalizing God's law, see "John Calvin's Three Uses of God's Law" (p. 88).

❺ Listen for the gospel.
This will come in the form of a sentence most likely starting with the name Jesus and ending with the words *for you.* Upon hearing the gospel, you may feel a physical lightness, as though you've set down a great burden. You may cry tears of joy. This is a fine response to the Word of God.

❻ End by saying, "Amen."
Since preaching is mostly God's work, honor the Word by sealing the moment with this sacred word, which means, "It is most certainly true!"

❼ Review.
If you've written notes, read through them later that day or the next day and consider corresponding with the preacher if you have questions or need clarification. If you've taken mental notes, review them in a quiet moment. Consider sharing this review time with others in your congregation or household on a weekly basis.

HOW TO RESPOND TO A DISRUPTION DURING WORSHIP

Disruptions during worship are inevitable. The goal is to soften their impact.

❶ Simply ignore the offending event, if possible. Many disruptions are brief and the persons involved act quickly to quiet them. Avoid embarrassing others; maintain your attention on the worship activity.

❷ Some disruptions cannot be ignored and may threaten to continue indefinitely. The agony will go on unless you act. Consider the following types:

Active Children

- *Your Problem:* You are most familiar with your own family. If you sense an outburst will end quickly, simply allow it to pass. If not, escort the child to the lobby for a little quiet time and then return. *Note:* Under all circumstances, children should be made to feel welcome in worship!

Try to ignore worship interruptions you think will end soon.

- *Someone Else's Problem:*
  Politely offer to help, perhaps by helping to occupy the child quietly or offering to escort the parent and child to the lobby, nursery, or cry room.

Personal Electronics

- *Your Problem:* Turn off cell phones, pagers, and other electronic devices immediately and discreetly. If you forget and a call comes through, switch off your phone immediately. Under no circumstances should you answer your phone during worship.

- *Someone Else's Problem:* Politely ask the person to respect worship by moving the conversation to the lobby.

Turn off all personal electronic devices before worship.

Chatty Neighbor

- *Your Problem:* Chatty persons should be alert to stares and grim looks from neighbors and be prepared to stop talking upon seeing them.
- *Someone Else's Problem:* Politely ask the talkers to wait until after worship to conclude the conversation. During the coffee hour, approach them with a cookie to mend any offense they may have felt.

Cameras

- *Your Problem:* If you would like to photograph an important event such as a baptism or profession of faith, ask first if cameras are allowed. If so, unobtrusively and discreetly position yourself out of the line of sight of other worshipers. Flash cameras are very distracting to the leaders, so avoid using a flash if at all possible.
- *Someone Else's Problem:* Politely offer to show the photographer where to stand to get the shot without obstructing worship.

Sound System Feedback

- Pastors often make jokes to cover for feedback and keep the appropriate mood for worship. If this happens, consider making a donation earmarked "for a new sound system."

Be Aware

- Some people perceive tennis shoes with light-up soles on worship leaders and praise team members as disruptive. If possible, coordinate the color of the shoe lights with the season of the church year to avoid undue flak.

- Plunging necklines, tight tops, and below-the-navel hip-huggers for females are designed to attract attention. They work; just ask any boy. Yet in worship—as in all of life—we aim to attract God's attention, but not with our clothes. Modest, comfortable clothing is appropriate for both sexes!

THE ANATOMY OF A BAPTISM

Sprinkling or pouring water on the baptized person, the pastor says, "I baptize you in the name of the Father, and of the Son, and of the Holy Spirit."

God is the true actor in baptism, bringing everyone involved to the font and inspiring trust and faith. Parents promise to teach their children about God and to raise them in God's ways. The whole congregation joins in these promises and pledges their support also.

Note: Reformed churches baptize people of all ages, not just infants. In the case of older children or adults, baptism is given only if those persons have consciously said they believe in Jesus Christ. When babies are baptized, the parents believe God has "graciously included them in his covenant and therefore they ought to be baptized." If you don't understand what baptism means in these cases, or if you wonder about baptizing babies, be sure to ask your pastor or an elder.

After the baptism, the pastor may trace the cross on the baptized person's forehead, reminding all present that he or she belongs to Christ.

Baptism is received with a believing heart that trusts in God's word. In the case of infant baptism, the mature and believing child or young adult will confirm God's promises made earlier in baptism, thus recognizing that the Holy Spirit gives him or her faith.

Water is the earthly element in baptism. God uses water to symbolize the washing away of sin and the drowning of the "old self" in the baptized person. Water itself can't do it; only Christ's sacrifice and the cleansing power of God's Spirit. Baptism is received by God's gift of faith.

HOW TO RECEIVE COMMUNION

The Sacrament of Holy Communion (also called the Lord's Supper) is a significant event in Reformed worship. A few Reformed churches celebrate communion weekly, but most do so monthly or six times annually. All five senses are engaged in communion, and it is the most interactive part of the service. Local customs for receiving communion can be confusing or complex, so it's wise to pay attention and prepare.

❶ Determine which method of distribution is used.
Verbal directions or printed instructions will likely be given before the bread and wine (or juice) are distributed. The three most common methods for communion are *individual cups*, a *common cup*, or *intinction* or dipping the bread (see p. 39).

In many congregations elders serve the worshipers, who remain seated in pews or chairs. Worshipers pass the bread (either in small pieces on a plate or a loaf to be broken as it is passed) and hold a piece until all have been served. Then the pastor invites the congregation to partake: "Take, eat, remember and believe that the body of Jesus was given to forgive your sin." Next the elders pass trays with small glasses of wine and/or juice. Again, worshipers hold their glass until all have been served and the pastor gives a similar invitation to drink. You will usually find racks to receive the empty glasses directly in front of you. The resonant clatter of worshipers placing empty cups in those racks is one of the most evocative sounds ever associated with reserved Reformed worship practices, as it reminds believers that *together and individually* they have celebrated what Christ has done for them.

Some congregations commune at tables or groups gathered in certain places in the sanctuary. Some congregations practice "continuous communion" with bread and wine stations, and some do both. .

❷ For churches where communicants leave their seats:
- The elder or usher will direct you where to go to receive the elements of communion.

- Proceed to the communion station.

- Best practice is often simply to follow the person in front of you and do what they do.

- Offer to assist people who are elderly or who might have trouble walking forward.

Individual Cups

❶ Receive the bread.
Bread is commonly distributed in full loaf form or in small precut pieces. The server will offer you the bread, perhaps saying something like "Christ gave his life for you."

❷ Receive the wine or juice.
Take a filled cup from the tray held out by the server. The server may say, "Jesus shed his blood for you." Drink the wine or juice, reflecting for a moment on exactly what it cost Christ to forgive your sin—or as Psalm 103:12 says, "remove our transgressions as far as east is from west."

❸ Return the empty cup.
You may deposit your empty cup in a tray provided at the place of communion. Or you may carry the empty cup back to your seat and place it in the rack with small holes. Maybe you wondered what they were used for. Now you know!

Common Cup

❶ Receive the bread.
As previously explained.

❷ Receive the wine.
The wine will be served in a large cup or "chalice" as a sign of unity. Assist the server by placing one hand underneath the cup and the other hand on its side. Help the server guide the cup to your lips.

Note: Avoid leaving "backwash." Drink only one sip from the common cup. Remove your lips from the cup immediately after receiving the wine.

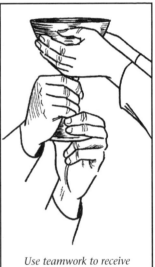
Use teamwork to receive the wine by common cup.

Intinction

Note: The word *intinction* is from the Latin word *intingere,* which means "to dip."

❶ Receive the bread.
Follow the same procedure as with individual cups and common cup, but *do not eat the bread yet.* If you acciden-

tally eat the bread prematurely, *remain calm*. Simply ask for another piece.

❷ Receive the wine.
Hold your piece of bread or wafer over the cup. Dip just the edge of it into the wine or juice. When the server says something like "The blood of Christ, shed for you," eat the wine-soaked bread.

❸ Do not panic if you accidentally drop your bread into the cup.
Again, the server can provide you with more bread. If the person distributing bread is too far away, the wine server may allow you to drink directly from the cup. Receiving only one element (bread *or* wine) is also considered full participation in communion.

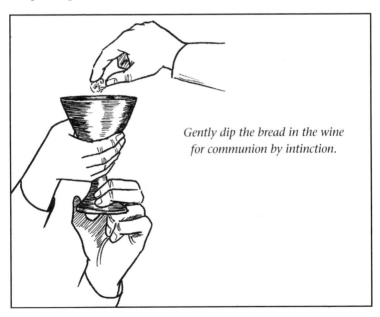

Gently dip the bread in the wine for communion by intinction.

Once You Have Communed

- *Return to your seat.* If communion is distributed in one continuous line, you may immediately return to your pew.

  OR

- *Wait for the completion of the distribution.* If you're being served as a group, you may need to wait until all other worshipers are served before returning to your seat. This is an appropriate time to close your eyes, pray, or listen to the communion music. Sometimes the communion will be served in deliberate silence.

- *Receive the post-communion blessing.* When everyone has been served, the presiding minister may bless the group, if he or she has not done so individually before.

- *Continue to participate when seated.* After returning to your place, you may join the congregation in singing the remaining communion hymns, or pray in silence.

Be Aware

- Many congregations offer the option of grape juice in addition to wine during communion. Verbal or written instructions will be given before distribution so you will be able to identify which chalice or cup contains grape juice.

- After receiving the bread and wine, avoid saying, "Thank you" to the server. The bread and wine are gifts from God. If you wish to respond, a gentle "Amen" or "Thanks be to God" is appropriate.

- Pastors may bless children or adults who are not communing, but who have come forward alone, with a companion, or with their family.

HOW TO PASS THE OFFERING PLATE

Passing the offering plate requires physical flexibility and an ability to adapt to differing practices. The offering is a practice that dates back to Old Testament times, linking money and personal finance directly to one's identity as a child of God. Giving of one's financial resources is an integral part of a healthy faith life.

❶ Pay close attention to instructions, if any.
The minister or a deacon may announce the method of offering and the cause for which it will be given. Instructions may be printed in the worship bulletin or projected on an overhead screen.

❷ Be alert for the plate's arrival at your row or pew.
Keep an eye on the deacons, if there are any. In most congregations, guiding and safeguarding the offering plate is their duty; wherever they are, there is the plate. As the plate approaches you, set aside other activity and prepare for passing.

❸ Avoid watching your neighbors or making judgments about their offering.
Many people contribute once a month by mail and some by automatic withdrawal from a bank account. If your neighbor passes the plate to you without placing an envelope, check, or cash in it, do not assume they didn't contribute.

❹ Place your offering in the plate as you pass it politely to the next person.
Do not attempt to make change from the plate if your offering is in cash. Avoid letting the plate rest in your

lap as you finish writing a check. Simply pass it on and hand your check to a deacon as you leave at the end of worship.

❺ Be sensitive to idiosyncrasies in offering plates or baskets.

Some congregations use wide-rimmed, felt-lined, chrome or brass-plated offering plates. Some use baskets of varying types. Some use cloth bags with handles that young children have mistaken for the wheel of a sailing ship, and which they have eagerly grabbed.

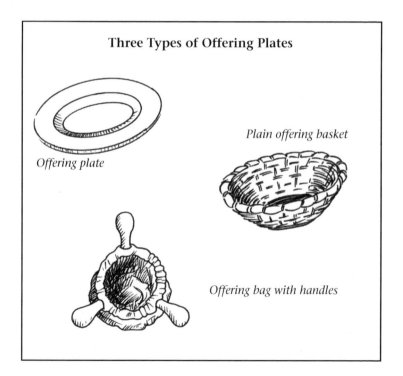

Three Types of Offering Plates

Plain offering basket

Offering plate

Offering bag with handles

Be Aware

- Some congregations place sturdy boxes for regular contributions to the church's budget at the entrances to the worship space.

- At least once a year someone—a deacon, a child, or an inattentive adult—dumps the offering bag, plate or basket. Coins roll; bills, checks, and envelopes fly all over like a flock of pheasant flushed by a retriever. Stay calm. Help pick up contents and return them to the plate.

- Your church offering may be tax deductible as provided by law. Consider making your offering by check or automatic withdrawal. You will receive a statement from your church in the first quarter of the next year.

- Churches often depend entirely upon the money that comes in through congregational offerings. If you are a member, resolve to work yourself toward tithing as a putting-your-money-where-your-mouth-is expression of faith. (The term *tithing* means "one-tenth" and refers to the practice of giving 10 percent of one's gross income to support the church's work.) Malachi 3—in the last book of the Old Testament—gives serious reasons for giving back to God what God has given to you.

- Everyone, regardless of age, has something to give— from wages; allowance; or babysitting, lawn-mowing, or car-washing money.

- Offerings are not fees or dues given out of obligation. They are gifts of thanksgiving returned to God from the heart.

HOW TO PASS THE PEACE IN CHURCH

In Romans 16:16, Paul tells members of the congregation to "greet one another with a holy kiss." The first letter of Peter ends, "Greet one another with a kiss of love. Peace to all of you who are in Christ" (1 Peter 5:14). Some Reformed people worry that this part of the worship service could turn into a free-for-all. Some also feel uncomfortable because of their fear of being hugged.

But think of it this way. Passing the peace usually comes near the beginning of worship—right after "God's greeting." Christians may—even *should*—greet each other with the peace of Christ because God first greets and welcomes us to worship. It's all about God. You can survive, and perhaps even embrace, the passing of the peace with these steps.

❶ **Adopt a peaceful frame of mind.**
Clear your mind of distracting and disrupting thoughts so you can participate joyfully and reverently.

❷ **Determine the appropriate form of safe touch.**
Handshaking is most common. Be prepared, however, for hugs, half-hugs, one-armed hugs, pats, and other forms of physical contact. Nods are appropriate for distances greater than two pews or rows. During flu season you may want to replace a handshake with a brief touch on a sleeve.

❸ **Refrain from extraneous chitchat.**
The passing of the peace is not the time for lengthy introductions to new people, comments about the weather, or observations about yesterday's game. A brief encounter is appropriate, but save conversations for the coffee hour.

❹ Make appropriate eye contact.
Look the other person in the eye but do not stare. The action of looking the person in the eye highlights the relationship brothers and sisters in Christ have with one another.

❺ Declare the peace of God.
"The peace of the Lord be with you," "Peace be with you," "The peace of God," "God's peace," and "The peace of Christ," are ways of speaking the peace. Once spoken, move on to the next person.

Be Aware
- Safe touch involves contact that occurs within your personal space but does not cause discomfort or unease.

Make good eye contact as you share God's peace with others.

HOW TO STAY ALERT
IN CHURCH

❶ **Get adequate sleep.**
Late Saturday nights are Sunday mornings' worst enemy.
Resolve to turn in earlier. A good night's sleep on Friday
night is equally important to waking rested on Sunday, as
sleep debt builds up over time.

❷ **Drink plenty of water, though not too much.**
It is easier to remain alert when you are well hydrated.
Take a small drink before worship but try not to leave
during the service to go to the bathroom unless it's a
necessity. Leaving worship is disruptive and discour-
teous—not just to other worshipers, but to God.

❸ **Eat a high-protein breakfast.**
Foods high in carbohydrates force your body to metabo-
lize them into sugars, which can make you drowsy. Try
eating oatmeal, Cream of Wheat, or Red River cereal or
eggs and grapefruit for a nutritious but light breakfast. If
you don't like oatmeal, ask your mom kindly not to make
you eat it.

❹ **Focus on your posture.**
Sit up straight with your feet planted firmly on the floor.
Avoid slouching, as this encourages sleepiness. Good
posture will promote an alert bearing and help you pay
attention so you'll get more out of worship.

❺ **If you have difficulty focusing on the service, divert
your attention. Occupy your mind, not your hands.**
Look around the worship space for visual stimuli. Keep
your mind active in this way while continuing to listen.

❻ Stay alert by flexing muscle groups in a pattern.
Clench toes and feet; flex calf muscles, thighs, buttocks, abdomen, hands, arms, chest, and shoulders. Repeat. Avoid shaking, rocking, or other movements that attract undue attention.

❼ If all else fails, consider pinching yourself.
Dig your nails into the fleshy part of your arm or leg or pinch yourself (*not* your pesky child or sibling). In extreme cases, bite down on your tongue with moderate pressure. Try not to draw blood or cry out.

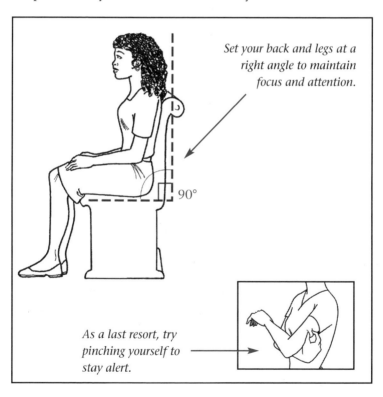

Set your back and legs at a right angle to maintain focus and attention.

90°

As a last resort, try pinching yourself to stay alert.

WHAT TO BRING TO A CHURCH POTLUCK (BY REGION)

It is a common practice in North American churches to enjoy three courses at potlucks (commonly referred to as "dishes"). Many of these dishes take on the flavor of the regions or cultures they represent. For best results, the preparer should understand the context in which the "dish" is presented.

The Salad

Potluck salads are quite different from actual salads. In preparation for making a potluck salad, ask yourself three questions:

- Is this dish mostly meat-free?
- Can this dish be served with a spoon or salad tongs?
- Can it be served chilled?

If the answer to any of these questions is yes, the dish is a potluck-eligible salad.

The Mixture

This is the foundation of any potluck salad. It gives the salad a sense of direction. If at all possible, use ingredients that are indigenous to your area. For example, broccoli, lettuce, apples, macaroni, and candy bars are common in more temperate climates. Always list ingredients to warn people with allergies. Stay away from nuts, even if a given recipe calls for them. Use garlic sparingly anywhere north of Chicago in the United States or Winnipeg in Canada.

The Crunchy Stuff

This component gives pizzazz to an otherwise bland salad. Examples: tortilla chips, shoestring potato crisps, onion crisps, pine nuts, sunflower seeds—or, for a joke that hardly any will get, fried pigskins.

The Dressing

This is the glue holds the salad together. The variety of available types is stunning, ranging from a traditional oil-based salad dressing to mayonnaise to non-dairy whipped topping. Use your imagination. Consult regional recipes for exact ingredients.

Note: Some salads are best when made well in advance and allowed to sit overnight. This is called *marinating,* or "controlled decomposition." Other salads are best prepared immediately before serving.

The Casserole

A three-layered dish, typically. In order to make each casserole as culturally relevant as possible, use the following guidelines. When in doubt, consult local restaurants for ideas.

Starch

East Coast: pasta or rice pilaf
Midwest: rice, potatoes, noodles, or more potatoes
South: grits or crumbled saltines lightly fried in margarine
Southwest: black, red, or pinto beans
North: wild rice
West Coast: tofu

Meat

East Coast: sausage or pheasant
Midwest: ground beef—in a pinch, SPAM® luncheon meat
South: crawdad, catfish, or marlin
Southwest: pulled pork
North: moose meat or walleye (pickerel in Canada) or any fish
in season
West Coast: tofu

Cereal

East Coast: corn flakes
Midwest: corn flakes
South: corn flakes
Southwest: corn flakes
North: corn flakes
West Coast: tofu flakes

Note: The starch and meat may be mixed with a cream-based
soup. The cereal must always be placed on the top of the
casserole, possibly with melted cheese.

Salad

Casserole

Dessert

The Dessert

The most highly valued dish at a potluck, this can be the simplest and most fun to make. There are two key ingredients:

1. flour
2. fudge

Regional influences can be quite profound. The following are examples of typical desserts around the continent. Consult your church's seniors for the nuances of your region.

Northern New Jersey: fudge brownies with fudge frosting

Sioux Centre, Iowa: triple-fudge fudge with fudge sauce and a side of fudge served on a square of raspberry Jello

Los Angeles: tofu fudge, fudge fortune cookies, or fudged fresh pineapple wedges

Chicago: large football-shaped blocks of solid milk chocolate, stamped with "Da Bears"

Toronto: fudge

Vancouver: cheesecake with fudge drizzle

Be Aware

- Use caution when preparing a dish. Adding local ingredients to any meat, salad, or dessert can increase the fellowship factor of your potluck exponentially. It also raises the risk of a "flop."

- Always follow safe food-handling guidelines.

- Any combination of flavored gelatin, shredded carrots, mini-marshmallows, and canned pears is an acceptable "utility" dish, should you be unable to prepare one from the above categories.

IMPORTANT THINGS THE REFORMERS WROTE AND WHY THEY'RE STILL IMPORTANT TODAY

❶ Sermons

Starting with Martin Luther, perhaps the most important work the reformers did was to change what pastors preached. Luther argued that God's Word had been held captive by bad preaching. By changing sermons to focus on proclaiming the gospel, Luther and the other reformers hoped to make sure God's promises could be freed to inspire people of faith. When that happened, people could actually come to know and trust Jesus as their Savior.

❷ Bible commentaries

John Calvin wrote a commentary (explanations and interpretations of Bible books) on every book of the Bible except Revelation. These often formed the bases of Calvin's daily lessons and weekly sermons in Geneva, Switzerland, where he served as "lead pastor" for all the churches (not just one congregation). Still in print today, Calvin's commentaries continue to be used by many pastors, scholars, and students, regardless of denomination.

❸ The Institutes of the Christian Religion

John Calvin wrote several editions of this monumental work beginning in 1534. Completing the last edition in 1555, Calvin organized it into four main sections or books. Many claim that the fourth book set the foundation for modern Christian social ethics and for the work

John Calvin's Bible commentaries and Institutes of the Christian Religion *are still in print today.*

of Christian social justice organizations and movements around the world.

❹ Confessional Documents

Many Reformed churches around the world hold similar beliefs that have developed into equally similar practices in worship, lifestyle, and practice of personal piety or devotions. The most familiar are "The Three Forms of Unity," which a number of Reformed denominations hold in common:

- *The Belgic Confession:* One of the oldest of the Reformed confessions. "Belgic" refers to what is the Netherlands and Belgium today and has nothing to do with rude manners. Guido de Brès was its main author in 1561. He was a preacher in the Netherlands Reformed churches and died a martyr in 1567. He wrote the Confession to protest oppression and persecution and to show that Reformed people were not rebels, as they were charged; instead they were law-abiding citizens who professed Christian doctrine according to the Bible.

- *The Heidelberg Catechism:* See introduction, page 199.

- *The Canons of Dort:* These consist of statements of doctrine adopted by the Synod (full church gathering) of Dort, meeting in Dordrecht, the Netherlands in 1618-19. This synod was held to settle a controversy in Dutch churches occasioned by the popular teachings of Jacob Arminius, a theological professor at Leiden University. He questioned John Calvin's teaching on the following important issues: election, limited atonement, total depravity, irresistible grace, the impossibility of falling from God's grace, and the perseverance of saints. These points are still today under discussion between Calvinists and Christians in the Baptist traditions.

In the year 1517 Martin Luther nailed his Ninety-five Theses to a church door in Wittenberg, setting the Reformation in motion. One of Luther's main attacks was against the sale of "indulgences," which claimed that people could buy their way into heaven.

FIVE THINGS YOU SHOULD KNOW ABOUT THE REFORMATION

❶ Most people in medieval times had low expectations.
They didn't know anything about advanced medicine, modern psychology, or what it was like to live in a democracy. They didn't expect to live very long. They didn't think they had much power over their lives. And they didn't think being an "individual" was very important.

❷ The reformers were Catholic.
The reformers wanted to make changes within the one Christian church in Europe, but they wanted to stay Catholic. None of them ever expected that their actions would lead to the hundreds of Christian denominations around today.

❸ People in medieval times weren't allowed to choose their own religion.
You could not believe whatever you wanted, but could practice only the faith your prince or king chose. After the Reformation, only the regions whose princes had signed the Augsburg Confession (an important Lutheran document) could practice any faith other than Catholicism.

❹ Martin Luther and John Calvin weren't the only reformers.
Luther and Calvin wanted the church to rediscover the good news of Jesus that creates and restores faith. Other reformers fought for these changes: separation of church and state, a personal relationship with God, better-educated clergy, and more moral leaders in the church.

❺ **The reformers cared about what you hear in church today.**
They taught pastors how to interpret and apply the Word of God obediently so it would hit home and create faith. This skill has been taught to Reformed pastors ever since.

FIVE FACTS ABOUT LIFE IN MEDIEVAL TIMES

❶ It lasted more than 1,000 years.
By some counts, the medieval period (or Middle Ages) began around the year 391 (when Christianity became the Roman Empire's only legal religion) and ended around 1517 (the year Martin Luther wrote the Ninety-five Theses).

❷ Life was nasty, brutish, and short.
People who survived childhood usually did not live much past forty. If disease or starvation didn't get you, violence and warfare did. It has been estimated that during the 1400s about one-third of Europe's population died of bubonic plague. Sanitation was practically nonexistent.

Road travel was harsh and sanitation was minimal during the Middle Ages.

❸ The Christian church grew larger, more influential, and more dominant.

Headquartered in Rome, the Western church became a superpower. Church and state became inseparable. At its height (ca. 1000-1300), "Christian Crusaders" battled Muslims and others for control of the "Holy Land," Thomas Aquinas wrote his *Summa Theologica*, and hundreds of "heretics" were burned to death.

❹ The "Cult of Saints" developed.

Over the centuries, a system grew in which the leftover good works (merits) of the saints could be distributed to others, with the pope in charge of this store (treasury) of good works. With his Ninety-five Theses, Martin Luther challenged this system.

❺ Humanist and Renaissance-age thinkers also worked for reform.

At the end of the Middle Ages, early reformers such as Jan Hus and Girolamo Savonarola confronted the church corruptions they saw. Hus was burned, and Savonarola was hanged. For other examples, see "History's Seven Most Notorious Heretics" on the next two pages.

HISTORY'S SEVEN MOST NOTORIOUS HERETICS

Though sometimes vilified by historians, heretics played a critical role in the church. They refined its message and forced the church to be honest with itself. Heretics usually suffered the death penalty—a high price for merely being wrong.

❶ Hypatia of Alexandria (370-415)
Hypatia was an African philosopher, mathematician, physicist, astronomer, and director of Alexandria's Library, once the largest in the world. Motivated by jealousy, Bishop Cyril of Alexandria declared her a heretic and ordered her tortured and burned at the stake, together with her writings. Her three major "mistakes": to prefer study to marriage, to know more than the bishop, and to be a female teacher of males.

❷ Pelagius (354-418)
Pelagius was a Celtic monk who believed in the goodness of human nature and the freedom of human will. These beliefs led him to denounce the doctrine of original sin—a core tenet of the church—and suggest that human beings were equal participants in their salvation with Jesus Christ. *Pelagianism* was an early form of self-help and self-reliance. When Pelagius taught that one could achieve grace without the church, he was excommunicated.

❸ Joan of Arc (1412-1431)
Joan was a French peasant girl who was able to hear heavenly voices that urged her to free her nation from British occupation. She was 19 when sentenced as a

heretic and burned at the stake. Joan's "mistake" was to be a better army leader than men. She is now a national hero and an official saint in the Roman Catholic Church.

❹ Girolamo Savonarola (1452-1498)
His parents wanted him to be a physician, but this Italian youngster decided to become a Dominican monk and serve people who were poor. He preached against Pope Alexander VI and the powerful Medici family. Members of the wealthy church and society hanged and burned him, then threw his ashes in the Arnos River to prevent him from having a resting place.

❺ Martin Luther (1483-1546)
Luther's father, a peasant and coal miner, wanted him to become a lawyer. Instead Martin became an Augustinian monk. Emperor Charles V and Pope Leo X threw him out of the church and put a price on his head. Regardless, Luther continued serving the poor, preaching and living the Bible, and sharing hospitality at the family dinner table.

❻ Hatuey (?-1511)
This Native American leader from the Guahaba region escaped from Haiti to Cuba. The brave Hatuey was captured and declared a heretic. A priest wanted to baptize him so that he would be able to get to heaven after being burnt. But the Taíno chief rejected the Christian rite when he heard that in heaven there would also be people from Spain. Today a brand of Cuban beer is named after Hatuey.

❼ Michael Servetus (1511-1553)

Servetus's heresy, trial, and death mark a low point in Calvinist history. A brilliant Spanish physician, he discovered that blood circulated from the heart to the lungs. Also a freelance theologian, his published views denying the Trinity and infant baptism incurred John Calvin's wrath. Curiosity brought Servetus to a church service in Geneva, Switzerland, where he was recognized and arrested. With evidence from Calvin, the Genevan Council convicted him of heresy and he was burned at the stake. Years later Genevan Calvinists erected an "expiatory monument" at the site to show their disapproval of violence as a deterrent to heresy.

HOW TO AVOID GETTING BURNED AT THE STAKE

Burning at the stake has a centuries-long history as punishment for heretics. (A heretic is someone who challenges established church teachings.) Some historians argue that many heretics have performed an essential function by forcing the church to clarify its position. Martin Luther himself was declared a heretic by the pope in 1521, when he would not recant his teachings; he survived under the protection of a friendly prince. While heretics are no longer treated in this way, it is nevertheless good to be prepared.

❶ Avoid public heresy.
Heresy is a formal public statement that disagrees with the church on an issue of dogma (official church teaching). Reformed churches were founded upon such statements. Martin Luther's Ninety-five Theses, for example, were considered heretical and entered as evidence against him at the Diet of Worms in 1521. ("Diet" is a now-rare usage meaning "legislative body" and has nothing to do with distasteful food.)

❷ Follow the proper channels if you are accused of heresy.
- Present your views to your local church council, session, or consistory.

- If they support you, ask them to present it to the regional deliberative body (classis or regional synod).

- If they do not support you, think really, really hard about going further.

- If you do decide to publicize your views further, follow the steps from the local, to the regional, to the national or international assemblies to which your denomination belongs.

- At every step, consider carefully arguments against your view. Are you sure you cannot be persuaded by the ever-broader assemblies that your views are unacceptable?

- If you accept the contrary judgment of any of those bodies, thank the church and your fellow believers for their patience and due process. Humbly return to your home church.

- If at every step your views are rejected, you will at some point likely be removed ("excommunicated") from the church because you no longer hold the views that you agreed to when you professed your faith publicly.

- Do not wage your battle endlessly by bad-mouthing those who disagreed with you. Instead find a church compatible with your view, even if not wholly in agreement.

- Oh yes—PRAY, PRAY, PRAY constantly for self-control, humility, wisdom, and the ability to respect those who disagree with you. If you started this process in the first place, you probably have a rebel streak that needs constant cleansing by God's Spirit. Rebel streaks aren't bad—all the reformers were rebels. But rarely are rebels saintly models of self-control and spiritual maturity.

❸ **Avoid practicing witchcraft.**
Witchcraft is considered a form of heresy since it depends upon powers other than God and the authority of the church. Practicing witchcraft does *not* include wearing Halloween costumes or reading books about wizards.

❹ Avoid getting nabbed in a political uprising—or be prepared to face the music.

Historically, persons who posed a political threat were sometimes burned at the stake. Or crucified.

Be Aware

- If you find yourself in a situation where being burned at the stake poses an imminent threat, wear flame-retardant clothing.

- If there is no hope of escape, request dry wood and plenty of dry kindling. Green wood burns slower, smokier, and at lower temperatures, causing a more painful death.

- Better yet, fake passing out soon after they light the fire. Maybe they'll cut you loose and throw you outside of town. Then wait till dark and run like mad.

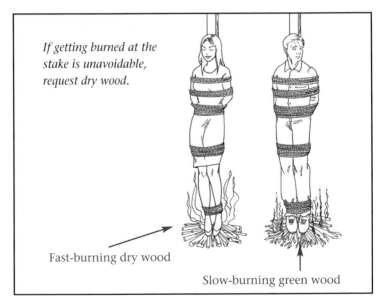

If getting burned at the stake is unavoidable, request dry wood.

Fast-burning dry wood

Slow-burning green wood

WORLD RELIGIONS

Listed by approximate number of adherents:

Christianity	2 billion
Islam	1.3 billion
Hinduism	900 million
Agnostic/Atheist/Non-religious	850 million
Buddhism	360 million
Confucianism and Chinese traditional	225 million
Primal-indigenous	150 million
Shinto	108 million
African traditional	95 million
Sikhism	23 million
Juche	19 million
Judaism	14 million
Spiritism	14 million
Baha'i	7 million
Jainism	4 million
Cao Dai	3 million
Tenrikyo	2.4 million
Neo-Paganism	1 million
Unitarian-Universalism	800,000
Rastafarianism	700,000
Scientology	600,000
Zoroastrianism	150,000
Toronto and Montreal hockey fans on 40 nights from October to April, plus play-offs	18,000+
University of Michigan and Ohio State University football fans respectively, every Saturday from September through December	100,000

COMPARATIVE RELIGIONS

Founder and date founded	Baha'i	Buddhism	Christianity
	Bahá'u'lláh (1817-1892) founded Babism in 1844 from which the Baha'i grew.	Founded by Siddhartha Gautama (the Buddha) in Nepal in the 6th-5th centuries B.C.	Founded by Jesus of Nazareth, a Palestinian Jew, in the early 1st century A.D.
Number of adherents in 2000	About 7 million worldwide; 750,000 U.S. 18,000 Canada.	360 million worldwide; 2 million U.S. 300,300 Canada.	About 2 billion worldwide; 160 million U.S. 22.8 million Canada.
Main tenets	The oneness of God, the oneness of humanity, and the common foundation of all religion. Also, equality of men and women, universal education, world peace, and a world federal government.	Meditation and the practice of virtuous and moral behavior can lead to Nirvana, the state of enlighten-ment. Before that, one is sub-jected to repeated lifetimes, based on behavior.	Jesus is the Son of God and God in human form. In his death and resurrection, he redeems humanity from sin and gives believers eternal life. His teachings frame the godly life for his followers.
Sacred or primary writing	Bahá'u'lláh's teachings, along with those of the Bab, are collected and published.	The Buddha's teachings and wisdom are collected and published.	The Bible is a col-lection of Jewish and Near Eastern writings spanning some 1,400 years.

Confucianism	Hinduism	Islam	Judaism
Founded by the Chinese philosopher Confucius in the 6th-5th centuries B.C. One of several traditional Chinese religions.	Developed in the 2nd century B.C. from indigenous religions in India, and later combined with other religions, such as Vaishnavism.	Founded by the prophet Muhammad, ca. A.D. 610. The word *Islam* is Arabic for "submission to God."	Founded by Abraham, Isaac, and Jacob ca. 2000 B.C.
6 million worldwide (does not include other traditional Chinese beliefs); U.S. and Canada uncertain.	900 million worldwide; 950,000 U.S. 297,000 Canada.	1.3 billion worldwide; 5.6 million U.S. 580,000 Canada.	14 million worldwide; 5.5 million U.S. 330,000 Canada.
Confucius's followers wrote down his sayings or *Analects*. They stress relationships between individuals, families, and society based on proper behavior and sympathy.	Hinduism is based on a broad system of sects. The goal is release from repeated reincarnation through yoga, adherence to the Vedic scriptures, and devotion to a personal guru.	Followers worship Allah through the Five Pillars. Muslims who die believing in God, and that Muhammad is God's messenger, will enter Paradise.	Judaism holds the belief in a monotheistic God, whose Word is revealed in the Hebrew Bible, especially the Torah. Jews await the coming of a messiah to restore creation.
Confucius's *Analects* are collected and still published.	The Hindu scriptures and Vedic texts.	The Koran is a collection of Muhammad's writings.	The Hebrew scriptures compose the Christian Old Testament.

FAMILY TREE OF CHRISTIANITY

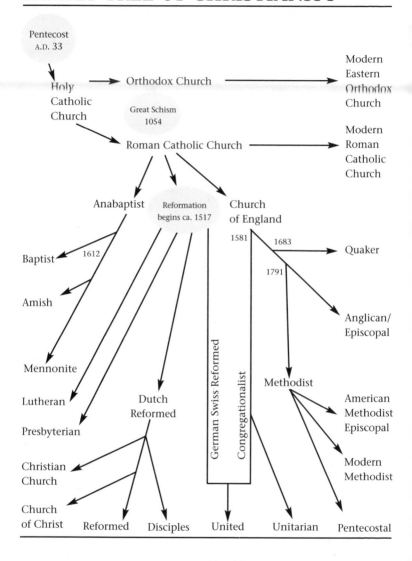

U.S. AND CANADIAN CHRISTIAN DENOMINATIONS

Listed by approximate number of adult adherents:

	United States	Canada
Catholic	66 million	13 million
Baptist	30 million	750,000
Methodist/Wesleyan	13 million	n/a in Canada; w/ UC of Can
Lutheran	9 million	600,000
Pentecostal/Charismatic	5 million	350,000
Orthodox	4 million	500,000
Presbyterian	4 million	409,000
United Church of Canada (UCC)	N/A	2.8 million
(a 1925 union of Congregational, Methodist, and Presbyterian denominations)		
Episcopalian/Anglican	3 million	2 million
Churches of Christ	3 million	
Congregational/ United Church of Christ	2 million	Part of Un. Ch. Canada
Assemblies of God Pentecostal Assemblies of Canada	1 million	250,000
Anabaptist	600,000	207,000
Reformed Church in America	300,000	6,300
Christian Reformed Church	200,000	76,000
Adventist	100,000	60,000

COMPARATIVE DENOMINATIONS

	Reformed/Presbyterian	Lutheran	Catholic
Founded when and by whom?	1536: John Calvin writes *Institutes of the Christian Religion.*	1517: Martin Luther challenges Catholic teachings with his 95 Theses. 1530: the Augsburg Confession is published.	Catholics consider Jesus' disciple Peter (died ca. A.D. 66) the first pope. Through Gregory the Great (540-604), papacy is firmly established.
Adherents?	**CRCNA** 300,000 (ca. 200,000 in U.S.; 76,000 in Canada); **RCA** 300,000 in U.S.; 6,300 in Canada; **Presbyterian** 40-48 million worldwide; 4 million U.S.	About 60 million worldwide; about 9 million U.S.; 600,000 in Canada.	About 1 billion worldwide; 66 million U.S.; 13 million in Canada.
How is Scripture viewed?	Protestant canon accepted. Scripture is the Word of God, inspired by the Holy Spirit, written in human words reflecting beliefs of the time, and is trustworthy in all it aims to teach.	Protestant canon contains 39 OT books, 27 NT. Scripture alone is the authoritative witness to the gospel.	The canon is 46 books in the OT (Apocryhpha included) and 27 in the NT. Interpretation is subject to church tradition.
How are we saved?	We are saved by grace alone. Good works result, but are not the basis of salvation.	We are saved by grace when God grants righteousness through faith alone. Good works inevitably result, but they are not the basis of salvation.	God infuses the gift of faith in the baptized, which is maintained by good works and receiving Penance and the Eucharist.
What is the church?	The body of Christ includes all of God's chosen and is represented by the visible church. Governed by regional "synods" or "classes" of elders.	The congregation of believers, mixed with the lost, in which the gospel is preached and the sacraments are administered.	The mystical body of Christ, who established it with the pope as its head; he pronounces doctrine infallibly.
What about the sacraments?	Although not necessary for salvation, baptism marks entry into Christ's body, the church; it confers Christian identity. The Lord's Supper is Christ's body and blood, which are really but spiritually present to believers.	Baptism is necessary for salvation. The Lord's Supper is bread and wine that, with God's Word, are truly Jesus' body and blood.	Catholics practice seven sacraments. Baptism removes original sin; usually infants. In the Eucharist bread and wine are changed into the body and blood of Christ by transubstantiation.

COMPARATIVE DENOMINATIONS

	Orthodox	Anglican	Methodist
Founded when and by whom?	A.D 330: Emperor Constantine renames Byzantium "Constantinople" and declares Christianity the empire's religion.	1534: Henry VIII is declared head of the Church of England. 1549: Thomas Cranmer produces the first *Book of Common Prayer*.	1738: Anglican ministers John and Charles Wesley convert. 1784: U.S. Methodists form a separate church body.
Adherents ?	About 225 million worldwide; about 4 million U.S.; 400,000 in Canada	45-75 million worldwide; about 3 million U.S.; 2 million in Canada	20-40 million worldwide; about 13 million U.S.; in Canada merged with most Presbyterians and Congregationalists in 1925 to form United Church of Canada.
How is Scripture viewed?	49 OT books (Catholic plus three more) and 27 NT. Scripture is subject to tradition.	Protestant canon accepted. Scripture is interpreted in light of tradition and reason.	Protestant canon accepted. Scripture is primary source for Christian doctrine.
How are we saved?	God became human so humans could be deified, that is, have the energy of God's life in them.	We share in the victory of Christ who died for our sins, freeing us through baptism to become living members of the church.	We are saved by grace alone. Good works must result, but do not obtain salvation.
What is the church?	The body of Christ in unbroken historical connection with the apostles; the Roman pope is one of many patriarchs who govern.	The body of Christ is based on "apostolic succession" of bishops, going back to the apostles. In the U.S., it is the Episcopal Church.	The body of Christ, represented by church institutions. Bishops oversee regions and appoint pastors, who are itinerant.
What about the sacraments?	Baptism initiates God's life in the baptized; adults and children. In the Eucharist, bread and wine are changed into body and blood, though there's no attempt to explain how.	Baptism brings infant and convert initiates into the church; in Communion, Christ's body and blood are truly present.	Baptism is a sign of regeneration; in the Lord's Supper, Jesus is really but spiritually present.

COMPARATIVE DENOMINATIONS

	Anabaptist	Congregational	Baptist
Founded when and by whom?	1523: Protestants in Zurich, Switzerland, begin believers' baptism. 1537: Menno Simons begins Mennonite movement.	1607: Members of England's illegal "house church" exiled. 1620: Congregationalists arrive in the New World on the *Mayflower*.	1612: John Smythe and other Puritans form the first Baptist church. 1639: The first Baptist church in America is established.
Adherents?	About 2 million worldwide; about 600,000 U.S.; 207,000 in Canada.	More than 2 million worldwide; about 2 million U.S.; in Canada merged with most Presbyterians and Methodists in 1925 to form United Church of Canada.	100 million worldwide; about 30 million U.S.; 750,000 in Canada.
How is Scripture viewed?	Protestant canon accepted. Scripture is inspired but not infallible. Jesus is living Word; Scripture is written Word.	Protestant canon accepted. Bible is the authoritative witness to the Word of God.	Protestant canon accepted. Scripture is inspired and without error; the sole rule of faith.
How are we saved?	Salvation is a personal experience. Through faith in Jesus, we become at peace with God, moving us to follow Jesus' example by being peacemakers.	God promises forgiveness and grace to save "from sin and aimlessness" all who trust him, who accept his call to serve the whole human family.	Salvation is offered freely to all who accept Jesus as Savior. There is no salvation apart from personal faith in Christ.
What is the church?	The body of Christ, the assembly and society of believers. No one system of government is recognized.	The people of God living as Jesus' disciples. Each local church is self-governing and chooses its own ministers.	The body of Christ; the redeemed throughout history. The term *church* usually refers to local congregations, which are autonomous.
What about the sacraments?	Baptism is for believers only. The Lord's Supper is a memorial of his death.	Congregations may practice infant baptism or believers' baptism or both. Sacraments are symbols.	Baptism is immersion of believers, only as a symbol. The Lord's Supper is symbolic.

COMPARATIVE DENOMINATIONS

	Churches of Christ	Adventist	Pentecostal
Founded when and by whom?	1801: Barton Stone holds Cane Ridge Revival in Kentucky. 1832: Stone's Christians unite with Disciples of Christ.	1844: William Miller's prediction of Christ's return that year failed. 1863: Seventh-Day Adventist Church is organized.	1901: Kansas college students speak in tongues. 1906: Azusa Street revival in L.A. launches movement. 1914: Assemblies of God organized.
Adherents?	5-6 million worldwide; about 3 million U.S.	About 11 million worldwide; about 100,000 U.S.; 60,000 in Canada.	About 500 million worldwide; about 5 million U.S.; 350,000 in Canada.
How is Scripture viewed?	Protestant canon accepted. Scripture is the Word of God. Disciples of Christ view it as a witness to Christ, but fallible.	Protestant canon accepted. Scripture is inspired and without error; Ellen G. White, an early leader, was a prophet.	Protestant canon accepted. Scripture is inspired and without error. Some leaders are considered prophets.
How are we saved?	We must hear the gospel, repent, confess Christ, and be baptized. Disciples of Christ: God saves people by grace.	We repent by believing in Christ as Example (in his life) and Substitute (by his death). Those who are found right with God will be saved.	We are saved by God's grace through Jesus, resulting in our being born again in the Spirit, as evidenced by a life of holiness.
What is the church?	The assembly of those who have responded rightly to the gospel; it must be called only by the name of Christ.	Includes all who believe in Christ. The last days are a time of apostasy, when a remnant keeps God's commandments faithfully.	The body of Christ, in which the Holy Spirit dwells; the agency for bringing the gospel of salvation to the whole world.
What about the sacraments?	Baptism is the immersion of believers only, as the initial act of obedience to the gospel. The Lord's Supper is a symbolic memorial.	Baptism is the immersion of believers only. Baptism and the Lord's Supper are symbolic only.	Baptism is immersion of believers only. A further "baptism in the Holy Spirit" is offered. Lord's Supper is symbolic.

THE SEASONS OF THE CHURCH YEAR AND WHAT THEY MEAN

Advent is a season of longing and anticipation, during which we prepare for the coming of Jesus. The church year begins with Advent, as life begins with birth, starting four Sundays before Christmas. The liturgical color for Advent is blue, which symbolizes waiting and hope. Some congregations light four "Advent candles"—one for each week—and a "Christ candle" on Christmas.

Christmas is a day *and* a season when we celebrate God's coming among us as a human child: Jesus, Emmanuel (which means "God with us"). The liturgical color for Christmas is white, which reminds us that Jesus is the Light of the world. Christmas lasts for 12 days, from December 25 to January 5.

Epiphany is celebrated on January 6, when we remember the Wise Men's (or Magi's) visit to the Christ child. The color for Epiphany Day is white. During the time after Epiphany we hear stories about Jesus' baptism and early ministry. The color for these Sundays is sometimes white and sometimes green. On the last Sunday we celebrate the Transfiguration. The color for this day is white, and we hear the story of Jesus shining brightly on the mountaintop.

Lent is a season when we turn toward God and think about how our lives need to change. This is also a time to remember our baptism, and how that gift gives us a new start every day! The color for Lent is purple, symbolizing repentance. Lent begins on Ash Wednesday and lasts for forty days (not including Sundays) and ends on the Saturday before Easter Sunday.

The Three Days are the most important part of the Christian calendar because they mark Jesus' last days, death, and resurrection. These days (approximately three 24-hour periods) begin on Maundy Thursday evening and conclude on Easter evening. On *Maundy Thursday* we hear the story of Jesus' last meal with his disciples and his act of service and love in washing their feet. On *Good Friday* we hear of Jesus' trial, crucifixion, death, and burial. On *Saturday*, at the nighttime *Easter Vigil*, we hear stories about the amazing things God has done for us. It is a night of light, Scripture readings, baptismal remembrance, and communion. On *Easter Sunday* we celebrate Jesus' resurrection and our new lives in Christ. Easter falls on a different date each year—sometime between March 22 and April 25.

Easter is not just one day but a whole season when we celebrate the resurrected Jesus. The season begins on Easter Sunday and lasts for fifty days (including Sundays). The color is white, symbolizing resurrection and joy. The Day of Pentecost falls on the fiftieth day of the season (*Pentecost* means fiftieth), when we celebrate the pouring out of the Holy Spirit and the church's mission in the world. This day uses the fiery color of red.

Ascension Day falls (!!) on the fortieth day after Easter and celebrates Jesus' return to heaven where "he sits at the right hand of the Father."

Time after Pentecost is the longest season in the church calendar, lasting almost half the year. Sometimes this is called "ordinary time" because there aren't many special celebrations during these weeks. The liturgical color for the time after Pentecost is green, representing life and growth. For congregations that follow the lectionary (weekly

Scripture readings from the Old Testament, psalms, gospels and epistles/letters) we hear stories about Jesus' ministry from one of the four gospels.

Special festivals are celebrated throughout the year. Some festivals occur the same time every year, such as Prayer Day for crops, Thanksgiving Day, Reformation Sunday (last Sunday in October), New Year's Eve, and New Year's Day. The color for these days is either white or red.

THE SEASONS
OF THE CHURCH YEAR

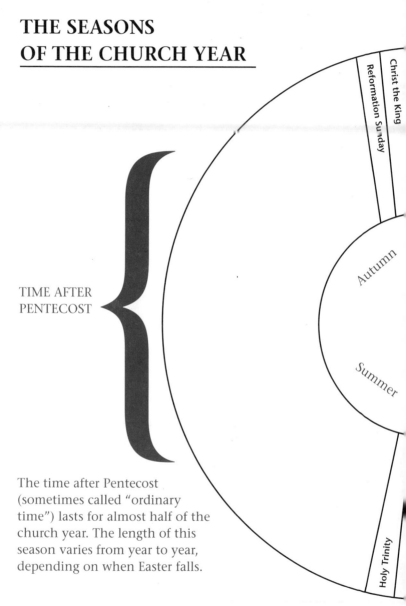

TIME AFTER
PENTECOST

The time after Pentecost
(sometimes called "ordinary
time") lasts for almost half of the
church year. The length of this
season varies from year to year,
depending on when Easter falls.

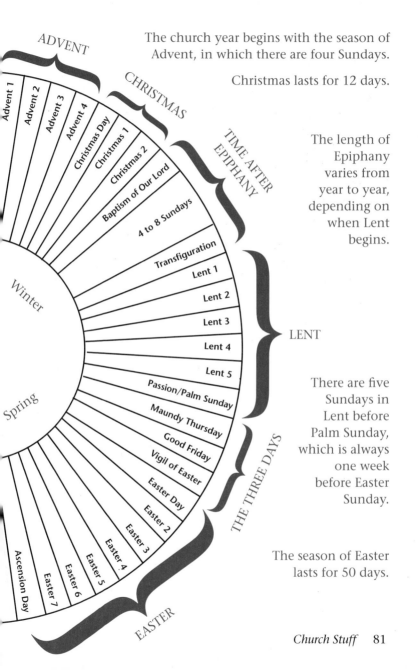

The church year begins with the season of Advent, in which there are four Sundays.

Christmas lasts for 12 days.

The length of Epiphany varies from year to year, depending on when Lent begins.

There are five Sundays in Lent before Palm Sunday, which is always one week before Easter Sunday.

The season of Easter lasts for 50 days.

ADVENT

CHRISTMAS

TIME AFTER EPIPHANY

LENT

THE THREE DAYS

EASTER

Advent 1
Advent 2
Advent 3
Advent 4
Christmas Day
Christmas 1
Christmas 2
Baptism of Our Lord
4 to 8 Sundays
Transfiguration
Lent 1
Lent 2
Lent 3
Lent 4
Lent 5
Passion/Palm Sunday
Maundy Thursday
Good Friday
Vigil of Easter
Easter Day
Easter 2
Easter 3
Easter 4
Easter 5
Easter 6
Easter 7
Ascension Day

Winter

Spring

MARTIN LUTHER

Martin Luther (1483–1546) spearheaded the Reformation by raising important questions about the church and translating the Bible for everyday people.

JOHN CALVIN

John Calvin (1509–1564) followed most of Luther's thought, but differed significantly on his understanding of sacraments and use of God's law.

CALVIN'S WORDS IN A MOTTO AND SEAL

"Cor meum tibi offero Domine prompte et sincere."

"I offer my heart to you, Lord, promptly and sincerely."

This motto and variations of the seal adorn many Reformed institutions and appear on books, letterheads, and diplomas. Though Calvin himself never used these exact words as a personal motto, it finds its origin in a letter he wrote to Guillaume Farel in August 1541. Farel had urged him to return from Geneva to Strasbourg. Having sacrificed his happy years in Strasbourg to answer God's call to Geneva, Calvin wrote, "When I remember that I am not my own, I offer up my heart presented as a sacrifice to God."

The heart and hand in this modern seal are surely noble depictions of the devotion to which all Christians should aspire. Yet they are really too lovely to portray the agony with which Calvin first wrote or the flawed nature of any human devotion to God. It might be more accurate to portray a broken, perhaps even bleeding heart, to show the agonized willingness with which many Christians before and since Calvin have lived in situations of stress, uncertainty, even persecution.

We think, for example, of Guido De Brès's 1562 letter to King Philip II that accompanied a copy of his Belgic Confession. De Brès declared that the confessors of the Reformed teachings summarized in the Confession were ready to obey the government in all lawful things, but that they would "offer their backs to stripes, their tongues to knives, their mouths to gags, and their whole bodies to the fire," rather than deny the truth expressed in this confession. De Brès himself was imprisoned and hanged for his faith in 1567 during this violent time of struggles between Roman Catholics and Protestants.

Rarely do Christians in North America or Western Europe have opportunities to stand so boldly for our faith these days. Yet we can, with God's grace, promptly and sincerely offer our hearts and lives—not losing heart but continuing to pray and to do our best, knowing that God does accept and bless our modest, clumsy, bungling, misshapen "heart-work." Through Christ, that heart offering is redeemed and made beautiful.

EVERYDAY STUFF

Believing in God involves more than going to church and reading the Bible. It's about keeping your faith with you in every part of your life. This section includes:

- Advice for helping people in times of trouble.

- Tips on forgiving others and treating them with respect—even if you don't always feel like it.

- Suggestions for avoiding temptation on a daily basis. Some of these ideas go back to the Middle Ages.

JOHN CALVIN'S "THREE USES OF GOD'S LAW"

One of the better-known elements of Reformed thought and life is John Calvin's comprehensive understanding of "God's Law." (He wrote extensively about this in Book II, chapter vii, section 12 of *The Institutes*.) For Calvin the Law is more than the Ten Commandments. It is the entire system of life and religion that God revealed to Moses. Because it is God's Law, it is perfect, as Psalms 19 and 119 affirm. Thus fallen people cannot keep it. As the apostle Paul observed about humanity, "All have *sinned* and fall short of the glory of God" (Romans 3:23).

So, what good is the Law? Reformed and Lutheran believers significantly agree about how God's Law is still useful.

- First (second according to Lutherans), because of its clarity and perfection, the Law acts as a "teacher." It shows us our own sinfulness and thus points us toward Christ—who alone kept the Law perfectly.

- Second, it still forms an ethical framework that curbs bad behavior. Even though we cannot keep this Law, it provides the point of reference for distinguishing good from evil. Calvin calls this the "political" use of the Law.

- The third use of God's Law is particularly for Christ-believers in whose hearts the Spirit of God already flourishes. For those people the Law guides their entire lives in a God-ward direction. This third use is the foundation for the third part of The Heidelberg Catechism, Q&A 91-115.

HOW TO SHARE YOUR FAITH WITH SOMEONE

Sharing the gospel with others is a natural part of exercising a mature faith. In fact, Jesus commanded his followers to do this, making it an important part of the life of faith (Matthew 28:18-20). Still, Reformed people tend to be rather shy evangelists.

While *evangelism* has become a negative word for some people, sharing the story of salvation in Jesus Christ is still the most rewarding way to live out one's faith. It is also a discipline that takes practice. Here are a few tips:

❶ Look for the opening.
Regular daily conversations offer many chances to talk about your faith. Listen for open-ended comments, such as, "I wonder why life is like that," or, "Sometimes life seems so hard." When possible, offer a response from a Christian perspective. Begin sentences with phrases such as, "I've come to think . . ." or, "I don't have the perfect answer, but I believe . . ."

❷ Be yourself.
Expressing your faith should be natural and the same as other types of daily conversation. Avoid suddenly switching your tone of voice or vocabulary. Also, don't try to impress the other person with your knowledge. Allow the Holy Spirit to guide you.

❸ Watch for a chance to take the conversation deeper.
Carefully gauge the other person's response. Observe his or her facial expression, verbal tone, and body language. If he or she seems to be closing down, set the topic aside and wait for another time. If he or she keys in and perks up, be prepared to continue.

❹ Open up.
Human beings are attracted to each other by our strengths, but we bond because of our weaknesses. Key to sharing your faith is the willingness to be honest about your own struggles. This will communicate safety, which for many people is critical.

❺ Shut up.
Don't monopolize the conversation, trying to save your friend by talking him into conversion. Always be sure to allow space and time for responses.

❻ Follow up.
Offer to continue the conversation later and arrange a time. At this point, the conversation will have become personally valuable to you. Allowing the person to see your commitment to your faith alongside your continuing questions will reassure him or her of your sincerity.

❼ Offer to share your faith community with the other person.
Most people join a church after being invited by a friend. When the time is right, invite the person to attend with you. Tell the person what makes it special to you.

❽ Try to maintain the relationship regardless of what the person does.

Be prepared for the other person to shut down around faith talk, decline your invitation to attend church, or even appear to avoid you. The most effective way to communicate that you're a follower of Jesus Christ is through your actions. Continue to live naturally and with integrity. Watch for another opportunity to open the subject later on.

HOW TO PRAY

Prayer is intimate communication with God and can be done before a meal, at bedtime, during a worship service, or any time the need or opportunity arises. Silent and spoken prayers are both fine and may be used liberally throughout the day. Prayer is also taking time to listen to what God is saying to us. Spontaneous prayer is often best, but the following process may help build the habit.

❶ Assess your need for prayer.
Take stock of the situation at hand, including your motivations. What are you praying for and why?

❷ Select a type of prayer.
There are many ways to pray, but it is helpful to practice a discipline or pattern to make your conversation with God whole-hearted and comprehensive. An easily remembered pattern is ACTS, with each letter describing and suggesting a distinct element of prayer:

- **Adoration:** This is another word for "worship." We worship God for who God is by recognizing and praising such things as God's greatness, justice, power, mercy, and the mystery and awesomeness of God's very existence.

- **Confession:** Because of who God is, we may pour out our hearts to God, confessing our sinful desires and acts and trusting that God will forgive us and set us straight.

- **Thanks:** Christians believe that everything we have and can do are gifts from God that we must use carefully for the benefit of others. Just as courteous people write thank-you notes for gifts received, we should thank God for our gifts.

- **Supplication:** This fine old word literally means "kneeling," but has come to mean a humble, honest request or petition. What better way to ask God for what we need than to kneel? (See below.)

❸ Select a physical prayer posture.
Many postures are appropriate:

- The most common type of prayer in the New Testament is from a prone position, lying face-down on the ground, arms spread.

- Kneeling with your face and palms upturned is good for prayers of supplication.

- Bowed head with closed eyes and hands folded is common today and aids concentration.

- There is no "official" posture for prayer. Choose your posture according to your individual prayer needs.

Choose a comfortable and appropriate prayer posture for your prayer time.

❹ Offer your prayer.
Pray with confidence. God listens to all prayer.
Breathe deeply, relax, and be open as the Spirit leads
you. Remember that even the apostle Paul recognized
that prayer was mysterious but effective and good
conversation with God. In Romans 8:26 he writes, "The
Spirit helps us in our weakness, for we do not know how
to pray as we ought, but that very Spirit intercedes with
sighs too deep for words."

❺ Listen.
Take time during your prayer simply to listen. Some
prayer traditions involve only silent meditation as a
means of listening for God's voice.

Be Aware

- God hears every prayer.

- Prayer can be done either alone or in the company of
  others, such as during the "Prayers of the People" in worship services or when we pray The Lord's Prayer at home
  or in worship.

HOW TO WORK FOR PEACE AND JUSTICE ON BEHALF OF PEOPLE WHO ARE POOR AND OPPRESSED

Reformed churches operate many agencies dedicated to social justice, community development, and disaster relief in different parts of the world. Two of them are listed below. Both of these agencies organize emergency disaster relief to assist people after floods, earthquakes, drought, or war. As well, they seek public policies to benefit hungry and poor people.

- Reformed Church World Service (www.rcws.rca.org) was formed in 1944 to help people after World War II. One distinctive feature today is its work to alleviate hunger and poverty with many partners that share that goal. RCWS helps people and communities develop long-term solutions to hunger, poverty, and health-related illness. RCWS provides funds to restock goat herds, provide tree seedlings, supply mosquito nets to reduce the incidence of malaria, and furnish desks, chairs, and school supplies for children.

- Christian Reformed World Relief Committee (www.crwrc.org) was organized in 1960 as a church response to natural disasters. One major goal of its ministry is community transformation. CRWRC's staff members live and work in 30 countries. They partner with more than 130 churches and community organizations to train local people to be leaders in their own communities.

- CRWRC and these partners help people work together to overcome illiteracy, hunger, malnutrition, unemployment, HIV/AIDS, child mortality, injustice, and other issues affecting them.

❶ Include people who are poor and oppressed in your daily prayers.

Keeping the needs of others in mind, especially people who suffer as a result of economic inequality, political oppression, or natural disaster, defines a person's good works. Name specific situations in your prayers and use specific place names and people's names whenever possible. Keep the newspaper on your lap as you pray, if necessary.

❷ Include people who are poor and oppressed in your personal or household budget.

Dedicate some of your personal giving to economic aid organizations. Learn something about the many causes and organizations that your congregation supports by asking your deacons or researching websites. Almost all congregations administer a "benevolence fund" to help support needy families both in and outside of the congregations. (Did you know the word "benevolence" literally means "wishing someone well"? God does that for us so we can do it for others too.)

❸ Pay close attention to economic and political conditions in other nations.

You can't help if you don't know what's really going on. Resolve to be a well-informed person who tests the worldview in the news against the worldview in the Bible. Use the Internet to locate independent and alternative news sources with unique, on-the-spot perspectives.

❹ **Get to know organizations that work for justice locally.**
Your congregation probably already organizes to do justice work in your neighborhood. If not, consider taking responsibility to organize a ministry team in your church. Several organizations with deep Reformed roots in the U.S. and Canada promote development of non-partisan thought and action in political, economic, and social arenas. Among them are the Association for Public Justice (Washington, D.C.), Centre for Public Justice (Ottawa, Ontario), and the Christian Labor Association (offices in the U.S. and Canada). The Christian Reformed Church's Office of Social Justice and Hunger Awareness works in both nations to inform congregations about justice-related themes and promotes advocacy on a wide variety of national and international issues.

❺ **Make working for justice part of your weekly or monthly routine.**
Devote a portion of your time regularly to a specific activity that personally connects you to people who are poor and disenfranchised. There is no substitute for personal contact.

❻ **Vote your conscience.**
If you are of voting age, remember that nations will be judged by the way they treat people who are disadvantaged. Keep this in mind when you go to your polling place.

❼ **Advocate for a cause in which you believe, one that has meaning for you personally.**
Perhaps you have a family member or close friend working in urban missions or in relief and development overseas. Ask such persons what you can do to promote their work in your community and church.

HOW TO IDENTIFY
A GENUINE MIRACLE

The term *miracle* describes something that causes wonder.
It is usually used in reference to an event that defies logical
explanation and appears to be the work of a higher force,
suggesting a reality beyond the five senses.

❶ **Disregard most minor situations.**
The facts should indicate a situation of high order, such
as one that is life-threatening, one involving suffering,
or one involving an immediate threat. Finding your
lost keys does not necessarily constitute a miracle.

❷ **Look for a lack of predictability.**
A positive outcome should be needed and wanted, but
not expected. Miracles tend to occur "out of the blue"
rather than as the result of an earthly cause, especially a
human one.

❸ **Evaluate the outcome.**
Miracles achieve a life-giving purpose; they never occur
outside the will of God. Suffering is relieved, God is
glorified, Jesus' presence is made manifest, the lowly are
lifted up, evil is thwarted, creation is revealed, or life is
saved. The outcome *must* be regarded as good, according
to biblical standards.

❹ Be appropriately suspicious about human claims to do miracles.

To make a miracle happen or to guarantee the results is beyond human ability. Often the event will defy what we know to be true about laws of nature or probability. If anyone takes credit for a supposed miracle or stands to make money or to advance an agenda from it, you are probably witnessing at best a hoax and likely a blasphemy.

❺ Adopt a wait-and-see perspective.

A miracle will still be a miracle later on. Labeling something a miracle too quickly could lead down unhelpful paths. Waiting to make the call while pondering the event in your heart will enhance your faith journey.

Be Aware

- The most overlooked miracle is that God shows up in everyday lives and provides so faithfully for our daily needs.

- The miracle of eternal life in Jesus Christ is a daily event and should be regarded as a free gift.

THREE ESSENTIAL PERSONAL SPIRITUAL PRACTICES

A spiritual practice or discipline is a routine for building one's faith. It involves actions and words that work together to center one's daily life in Jesus Christ. Medical studies show that people who pray regularly throughout the day suffer less stress, have lower incidence of heart disease, and live longer on average than those who do not.

But how do you get into the habit of regular piety? Try this: Write "God" in your daily schedule at the same time six days a week for two months. (It's OK to take a day of rest from personal devotions.) If you're like most North Americans, you schedule your life to the minute and rarely miss appointments. Guess what? God *never* misses an appointment. God will show up, even if you don't. Pretty soon you won't have to put the time down; it will be a habit.

❶ Morning Devotions

- Right after awakening, turn your attention first to God. The silence and solitude available in the morning hours are ideal.

- Try to make prayer the first activity of your day. If necessary, set your alarm to sound 15 minutes early to give yourself time.

- Read a psalm or two—these are the Bible's own prayer book.

- Begin with thanks and by remembering God's constant presence.

- Identify events you anticipate in your day and how you feel about them.

- Ask God to provide what you need for the day.

- Pray on behalf of other people. Keep a list of names or prayer items tucked inside your Bible or devotional book.

- Finish your devotions by reading from the Bible, a devotional book, or a spiritual reading. Your pastor, church librarian, or local Christian bookstore can make good suggestions.

- A whole pattern for prayer can be read from a prayer book. (This is especially helpful to couples.) Ask your pastor to suggest an appropriate prayer book.

❷ Mealtime Grace
Human beings naturally pause before a meal. Use those moments to give thanks and ask for a blessing.

- Consider establishing mealtime grace as a household ritual.

- When eating in public, be considerate of others, but do not abandon your practice.

- Once your meal is assembled and ready to eat, take time before praying to gather your thoughts and call an appropriate prayer to mind.

- Many people say a memorized prayer at mealtimes, such as the Lord's Prayer. Consider occasionally departing from your regular prayer with an extemporaneous one.

Praying before mealtime is a great personal ritual that can be shared with others.

Here are a few examples of mealtime graces. Some of these prayers can be sung to tunes that vary from place to place.

- We thank thee for the morning light, for rest and shelter all the night, for health and food and love and friends—for everything thy goodness sends. Amen.

- God is great and God is good. Now we thank him for our food. By his hand we all are fed. Grant us, Lord, our daily bread. Amen.

- Lord Jesus, be our holy guest, our morning prayer, our evening rest. And with this daily food impart thy love and grace to every heart. Amen.

- For food in a world where many walk in hunger; for faith in a world where many walk in fear; for friends in a world where many walk alone—we give you humble thanks, O Lord. Amen.

- Thank you, Lord, for food and drink and friendship. Bless our table, deepen our gratitude, broaden our sympathies, and strengthen our service in your love. Amen.

- Lord, bless us sinners as we eat our dinners.

- *Por estos bienes, O Señor, te damos gracias hoy.* For these good things, O Lord, we give you thanks today.

❸ Evening Prayer

The other daily rituals you perform in the evening, like brushing your teeth or letting the cat out, create a natural structure for evening prayer.

- Establish a regular time, such as sunset or at bedtime, and commit to it.

- Confess wrongdoing and ask for forgiveness.

- Tell God about the joys and sorrows of the day. Ask for help with the sorrows and give thanks for the joys.

- Identify the good things about the day. On bad days, find at least one thing for which to give thanks.

- Consider using a devotional as a guide and companion.

- Think about involving other members of your household in this ritual. Evening prayer particularly can be enhanced through sharing, taking time before prayer to review your day's activities, making a list of things to frame into the ACTS pattern (see p. 92).

- Prayer books have a beautiful evening prayer called "Compline" that dates back to A.D. 400.

HOW TO FORGIVE SOMEONE

Forgiving is one of the most difficult disciplines of faith, since it seems to cost you something additional when you've already been wronged. Swallowing your pride and seeking a greater good, however, can yield great healing and growth.

❶ Acknowledge that God forgives you.
When you realize that God has already shown forgiveness and continues to forgive sinners like you, it's easier to forgive someone else.

❷ Consult Scripture.
Jesus taught the Lord's Prayer to his disciples, who yearned to become like he was. Forgiveness was a big part of this. Read Matthew 6:9-15.

❸ Seek the person out whenever possible.
Consciously decide to deliver your forgiveness in person. In cases where this is geographically impossible, find an appropriate alternative means, such as the telephone.

Note: This may not be wise in all cases, given the timing of the situation, the level of hurt, or in cases where abuse has taken place. Certain problems can be made worse by an unwelcome declaration of forgiveness. Consult with a pastor before taking questionable action.

❹ Say, "I forgive you," out loud.
A verbal declaration of forgiveness is ideal. Speaking the words enacts a physical chain reaction that can create healing for both speaker and hearer.

❺ Pray for the power to forgive.

Praying for this is always good, whether a forgiveness situation is at hand or not. It is especially helpful in cases where declaring forgiveness seems beyond your reach.

Be Aware

- When someone sins against you personally, forgiving him or her does not depend upon their feeling sorry (showing remorse) or asking for your forgiveness. But it helps. You may have to struggle, however, to forgive the person without his or her consent or participation.

- Forgiveness is not the same as reconciliation. It takes two or more to reconcile. It takes only one to forgive.

HOW TO CONFESS YOUR SINS AND RECEIVE FORGIVENESS

Anyone may confess and any believer may pronounce the word of forgiveness. A declaration of forgiveness is permanent and binding because it comes from Jesus Christ himself.

❶ Make a mental list of your offenses.

❷ Locate a fellow Christian.
When appropriate, confess your sins to another person (see James 5:16).

❸ Resolve to confess of your own free will.
Don't confess merely because someone else wants you to do it. Make your confession voluntarily.

❹ Make your confession fearlessly, aloud if possible.
Confess the sins that burden you, and then confess the sins of which you are not aware or can't remember.

❺ Avoid making up or skimming over sins.
More important than facts and figures is a spirit of repentance in your heart.

❻ Receive forgiveness as it is given, in the name of the Father and of the Son and of the Holy Spirit.
God forgives you fully. Psalm 103:8-13 movingly describes the breadth of God's forgiveness.

❼ Resolve to live joyfully and penitently.
With absolution comes new life in the freedom of God's grace.

Be Aware

- Unburdening your conscience through confession is cleansing and good for the soul; it's not meant to be torture.

- Ultimately, forgiveness comes from God. A perfect and pure confession is not a strict requirement to receive it.

Confess your sins to another Christian.

HOW TO DEFEND YOUR FAITH AGAINST ATTACK

Defending your faith from attack involves tact and savvy. You must be able to empathize with your adversary and use his or her affronts creatively without getting baited into an angry or hostile response. The Reformed theological perspective was hammered out in a context of debate and controversy, though you probably don't need to go looking for a fight nowadays. Just be ready. There is no substitute for knowing your stuff.

❶ Employ the 80/20 rule.
In any debate, it is best to listen at least 80 percent of the time and talk 20 percent of the time.

❷ Engage in active listening.
Active listening means to try to comprehend not just the content of another's position, but also the emotional thrust behind it. This is important especially in cases where the speaker's emotional expressions are intense.

❸ Restate your adversary's argument empathetically.
Use sentences like, "So, you're upset because Christians seem to say one thing and do another."

❹ Identify with what the speaker is saying.
For example, say, "I know what you mean. I see phony behavior at my own church." This elevates the conversation and keeps it civil.

❺ **Do your best to put the speaker at ease.**
Having made clear that you understand his or her position, you are free to state your defense or counterpoint. Offer "I statement" responses, such as, "I wonder how I would stand up under that kind of scrutiny myself," or, "I try my best not to judge others too harshly. I'd hate to be judged by those standards."

❻ **Keep it as upbeat as possible.**
Use humility, humor, and a pleasant nature to defuse any tension. Though hard to practice, it is possible to disagree with someone while remaining friends.

❼ **Give your opponent his or her due.**
When the speaker makes a good argument, say, "You make a good point." This will further elevate the conversation. If you still disagree, make your counterargument calmly.

❽ **Avoid closing off the conversation or leaving it on a sour note.**
If you can, offer to continue the discussion over a lunch that you buy. Avoid falling into a "winner-take-all" mind-set. Keep respect as your highest value.

Be Aware

• Don't try to argue the other person in or out of their point of view. Just respectfully and sincerely offer what you believe.

- Attacks on faith are not limited to verbal assaults, especially in countries such as China or Vietnam, where religious persecution is a reality. Take care when visiting such places, especially when distributing religious materials or sharing stories about your faith.

- It is best in all cases to avoid sounding smug or preachy where your points resemble counterattacks.

HOW TO RESIST TEMPTATION

We have inherited much good advice from Martin Luther. One thing we've lost is the down-to-earth, common sense ways that Luther advised people to resist temptation. These are ideas he gave people who said they were tempted.

❶ **Run the opposite direction.**
Learn to identify the things that tempt you and avoid situations in which temptation will occur. When you see a temptation coming down the road, take a detour.

Note: Promise Keepers discovered that more than 30 percent of *Christian* men have used pornography regularly over long periods. If that is your habit, first recognize that using it is yielding to the temptation to view other persons as sexual objects. Pray for the power to click it off and erase the URL from your computer and mind.

❷ **Laugh at the tempter.**
Temptations are simply things that want to gain power over you. When you laugh at them, you reduce them to their proper place.

❸ **Distract yourself with other healthier activities.**
God knows what's good for you and so do you. Find an alternate activity that promotes trust in God and requires you to care for your neighbors. Seek the company of others, especially people to whom you may be of service.

❹ **Remember that your Lord also confronted temptation.**
Jesus faced down temptation by telling the devil the truth, namely, only God is Lord. Consider using a contemporary version of Jesus' words: "God's in charge here, not you."

❺ Tell the devil to go back to hell.

Consider saying this: "You're right, Mr. Devil. I'm a sinner. But you have no power here. My Lord loves sinners and has forgiven me forever. There's nothing you can do about it. Go back to where you came from and quit bothering me!"

❻ Read Scripture and pray.

When Jesus was tempted (see Matthew 4:1-11 and Luke 4:1-13), he faced the devil with his knowledge of the Hebrew Scriptures (our Old Testament). The more you read the Bible, the better prepared you'll be to face your own temptation by falling back on God's Word instead of your own strength or knowledge. Pray for the Spirit's help in resisting temptation.

Even Jesus faced temptation when the devil confronted him in the wilderness.

Be Aware

- There are different kinds of temptation. Regardless of the type, temptation always involves a hidden voice whispering to you, "Whatever God says, you really need to trust me instead. I'm the only thing that can help you."

- Temptations try to make us trust in ourselves or in other things more than in God. When you realize this, you'll see that everything on the list above is just turning back to Jesus who died to show you how much you can trust him.

HOW TO CARE FOR THE SICK

While a trained and licensed physician must be sought to treat illness and injury, there is no sickness that cannot be helped with faithful attention and prayer.

❶ Assess the nature of the problem
Visit a local pharmacy if the illness is a simple one. Over-the-counter medications usually provide temporary relief until the body heals itself. If symptoms persist, the sick person should see a doctor and get a more detailed diagnosis.

❷ Pray for the sick.
Intercessory prayers are prayers made on someone else's behalf. Add the afflicted person to your church's prayer list.

❸ Call in the elders.
Prayer and emotional support from friends and family are vital parts of healing, living with illness, and facing death. Ask the pastor to assemble the church elders (leaders) for prayer and the laying on of hands. Here's what the Bible says on this topic: "Are any among you sick? They should call for the elders of the church and have them pray over them, anointing them with oil in the name of the Lord" (James 5:14).

Be Aware
• Many people claim expertise in healing, from acupuncturists and herbalists to "faith healers" and psychics. It's OK to be skeptical of such claims, but treat the practitioners respectfully.

- Many people believe that much healing can be found in "comfort foods," especially homemade chicken soup.

- Those who attempt to diagnose and treat their own symptoms often do more harm than good. When in doubt, always consult a pharmacist, doctor, or other medical professional.

Gather friends, family, and church leaders to pray and lay hands on sick people.

HOW TO IDENTIFY
AND AVOID EVIL

The devil delights in unnoticed evil. To this end, the devil employs a wide array of lies, disguises, and deceptions while attacking our relationships with God and each other. A sharp eye and vigilance are your best defense. Many Christians dislike openly discussing the subject of evil—except when they see it in others. Yet many secretly cultivate extraordinary talent for rooting it out and they can be helpful allies in the struggle against evil.

❶ **Know your enemy.**
Evil appears in many forms. Most often it camouflages itself as kindly or friendly or good. Cruelty, hatred, violence, and exploitation are also among the many forms evil can take, but it often masquerades as justice or something done "for their own good." Be alert to acts, people, and events that employ these methods, even if the eventual outcome appears good.

❷ **Proceed carefully and deliberately.**
Avoid rushing to conclusions. Use good judgment.

❸ **Take action to expose the evil.**
Evil relies on darkness. It wants to remain hidden and hates the light of truth. Things that suffer from public knowledge or scrutiny might be evil.

❹ **Be prepared to make a personal sacrifice.**
Fighting evil can be costly. A successful counterattack may require you to give up something you cherish. For Jesus, as for many of his followers, sacrifice was his lifestyle. Love is the foundation of sacrifice that combats evil.

❺ Stay vigilant.

Evil's genius is shown in disguise, deception, and misdirection. Maintain your objectivity and apply the biblical measures of right and wrong you know to be correct. Martin Luther's standard was a conscience informed by Scripture and good common sense.

HOW TO AVOID GOSSIP

Gossip is among the most corrosive forces within a community and should be monitored closely. Discovery of gossip should be viewed as an opportunity to defend your neighbor's integrity, both the gossiper and the victim of gossip.

❶ **Determine whether the conversation at hand qualifies as gossip.**
- Gossip involves one party speaking about a second party to a third party.

- The person who is the topic of gossip is not a participant in the conversation.

- The tone of the conversation is often secretive or negative. Gasps and whispers are common.

- The facts expressed in a gossip conversation are often unsubstantiated and have been obtained second- or third-hand.

❷ **Recall and obey Titus 3:2: "Speak evil of no one."**

❸ **Interject yourself into the conversation politely.**
Ask whether the gossiper(s) have spoken directly to the person about whom they are talking. If not, politely ask why. This may give some indication of why they are gossiping.

❹ **Make a statement of fact.**
Gossip withers in the face of truth. Make an attempt to parse out what is truly known from conjecture and

supposition. State aloud that gossip is disrespectful and unfair.

❺ Offer an alternative explanation based on fact.
Describe other situations that cast the victim of gossip in a favorable light. Always try to give people the benefit of the doubt.

Avoid gossip. It undermines community and damages relationships.

Be Aware

- There is a fine line between helping and meddling. Pay close attention to your own motivations and the possible outcomes of your actions.

- Gossip injures both the gossiper and the person who is the subject of rumors.

- Consult the Heidelberg Catechism's explanation of the ninth commandment (Q&A 112).

- For further help, look up James 4:11.

HOW TO RESOLVE INTERPERSONAL CONFLICT

Disagreements are part of life. They often occur when we forget that not everyone sees things the same way. Conflict should be viewed as an opportunity to grow, not a contest for domination. Many Reformed people are traditionally shy, but when push comes to shove they value healthy relationships above all.

❶ Adopt a healthy attitude.
Your frame of mind is critical. Approach the situation with forethought and calm. Prayer can be invaluable at this stage. Do not approach the other party when you're angry or upset. Yet remember the apostle Paul's good advice: "Do not let the sun go down on your anger" (Ephesians 4:46).

❷ Read Matthew 18:15-20 beforehand.
Consult the Bible to orient your thinking. This is the model Jesus provided and can be used to call to mind an appropriate method.

❸ Talk directly to the person involved.
Avoid "triangulation." Talking about someone to a third party can make the conflict worse, as the person may feel that he or she is the subject of gossip. Speaking with the other person directly eliminates the danger and boosts the odds of a good outcome.

❹ Express yourself without attacking.
Using "I statements" can avoid casting the other person as the "bad guy" and inflaming the conflict.

"I statements" are sentences beginning with phrases such as "I feel . . ." or "I'm uncomfortable when . . ."

⑤ Keep "speaking the truth in love" (Ephesians 4:15) as your goal.
Your "truth" may not be the other party's. Your objective is to discover and honor each other's "truth," not to put down the other person. Be ready to admit your own faults and mistakes.

⑥ Seek out a third party to act as an impartial witness.
If direct conversation doesn't resolve the conflict, locate someone both parties trust to sit in. This can help clarify your positions and bring understanding.

⑦ Build toward forgiveness and a renewed friendship.
Agree upon how you will communicate to prevent future misunderstandings.

When two people aren't getting along, sometimes an impartial third person can help resolve the dispute.

Be Aware

- Seemingly unrelated events in your or the other person's life may be playing an invisible role in the conflict at hand. Examine yourself and be ready to shift the focus to the real cause.

- You may not be able to resolve the conflict at this time, but don't give up on resolving it in the future.

HOW TO COMFORT SOMEONE

Comfort is a gift from God. Christians in turn give it to others to build up the body of Christ and preserve it in times of trouble or sadness. (See 2 Corinthians 1:4-7.) Reformed people often employ food as a helpful secondary means by bringing meals to friends or families during times of illness or other crisis.

❶ Listen first.
Make it known that you're present and available. When the person opens up, be quiet and attentive.

❷ Be ready to help the person face grief and sadness, not avoid them.
The object is to help the person name, understand, and work through his or her feelings, not gloss over them.

❸ Avoid saying things to make yourself feel better.
"I know exactly how you feel," is seldom true and trivializes the sufferer's pain. Even if you have experienced something similar, no experience is exactly the same. If there is nothing to say, simply stay present with the person for a reasonable time.

❹ Show respect with honesty.
Don't try to answer the mysteries of the universe or force your beliefs on the person. Recognize the limits of your abilities. Be ready to let some questions go unanswered. Consolation isn't about having all the answers; it's about bearing one another's burdens.

❺ Don't put words in God's mouth.
Avoid saying, "This is God's will," or, "This is part of God's plan." Unless you heard it straight from God, don't say it.

HOW TO COPE WITH LOSS AND GRIEF

Many Christians downplay very serious losses by saying, "Well, it could be worse." This may provide only temporary relief at best. Any loss can cause pain, feelings of confusion, and uncertainty. These responses are normal.

❶ Familiarize yourself with the stages of grief.
Experts identify five: denial, anger, bargaining, depression, and acceptance. Some add hope as a sixth stage. Grieving persons cycle back and forth through the stages, sometimes experiencing two or three in a single day. This is normal.

❷ Express your grief.
Healthy ways may include crying, staring into space for extended periods, ruminating, shouting at the ceiling, and sudden napping. It is very common for grieving people to gather together and tell stories about their friend or family member who has died. Often those stories are hilarious and provide healthy memories. Sometimes it is most appropriate to laugh even while mourning.

One of the best ways to help grandchildren who have lost a dear grandparent is to gather them in one room and ask each to tell a favorite story or memory of the person. Often children will be laughing and crying almost simultaneously as they continue building close family relationships even in their grief.

❸ Identify someone you trust to talk to.
Available people can include a spouse, parents, relatives, friends, a pastor, a doctor, or a trained counselor. Many household pets make good listeners and willing confidants.

❹ Choose a personal way to memorialize the loss.
Make a collage of photographs, offer a memorial donation to your church, or start a scrapbook of memories to honor the event. This helps you to begin to heal without getting stuck in your grief.

Even Jesus felt the loss of Lazarus when he died.

Mary   Martha

Be Aware

- Many experts prescribe a self-giving activity, such as volunteering at a shelter or soup kitchen, as a means of facilitating a healthy grieving process.

- The pain immediately after suffering a loss is usually deep and intense. This will lessen with the passage of time.

- Anger, guilt, bitterness, and sadness are likely emotions.

- Short-term depression may occur in extreme cases. After experiencing a great loss, such as the death of a loved one, make an appointment with your family physician for a physical.

- Even Jesus cried when his friend Lazarus died (John 11:35).

THE TOP TEN ATTRIBUTES TO LOOK FOR IN A SPOUSE

While no single personality trait can predict a compatible marriage, the following list frames the basic things to look for in a spouse. With all attributes, some differences can be the source of a couple's strength rather than a source of difficulty. Statistically, Reformed people appear to be about as successful at choosing a spouse as other people.

❶ Similar values.

Successful couples may be very different in personalities, but values that concern religious beliefs, life purpose, financial priorities, and children are a foundation on which to build the relationship. Contrary values tend to create discord.

❷ Physical energy and physical space compatibility.

Consider whether the person's energy level and physical space needs work with yours. Realize that *compatibility* can mean a complementary match of opposites, or it can denote a match based on strong similarities.

❸ Physical and romantic compatibility.

If the two of you have a similar degree of interest in or need for physical and romantic expression in your relationship, the chance of lifelong compatibility increases.

❹ Intellectual parity.

Communicating with someone who has a significantly different intelligence level or educational background can require extra effort.

⑤ Emotional maturity.
A lifelong relationship of mutual challenge and support often helps each person grow emotionally. A lifetime spent waiting for someone to grow up could be more frustration than it's worth.

⑥ Sense of humor.
A sense of humor can provide an excellent measure of a person's personality and an important means of couple survival. If he or she doesn't get your jokes, you could be asking for trouble.

⑦ Respect.
Look for someone who listens to you without trying to control you. Look also for a healthy sense of self-respect.

⑧ Trustworthiness.
Seek out someone who is honest and acts with your best interests in mind—not only his or hers—and who tries to learn from his or her mistakes.

⑨ Forgiving.
When you sincerely apologize to your spouse, he or she should try to work through and get beyond the problem rather than hold on to it. Once forgiven, past mistakes should not be raised, especially in conflict situations.

⑩ Kindness.
An attitude of consistent kindness may be the most critical attribute for a lifelong partnership.

Be Aware

- If you live to be old, you will probably experience major changes that you cannot predict at age 15 or 25 or 35. Accepting this fact in advance can help you weather difficult times.

- Use all of your resources—intuition, emotions, and rational thought—to decide about a life partner.

- Family members and trusted friends can offer invaluable advice in this decision-making process and should be consulted.

A sense of humor is an important means of couple survival.

SOME OF JOHN CALVIN'S KEY THOUGHTS ON SPIRITUAL LIVING

❶ On the knowledge of God.
Nearly all the wisdom we possess, that is to say, true and sound wisdom, consists of two parts: the knowledge of God and of ourselves. —*The Institutes* I.1.1

❷ On the Word of God.
It now remains to pour into the heart itself what the mind has absorbed. For the Word of God is not received by faith if it flits about in the top of the brain, but when it takes root in the depth of the heart that it may be an invincible defense to withstand and drive off all the stratagems of temptation. —*The Institutes* III.2.36

❸ On believers' mysterious union with Christ.
Not only does Christ cleave to us by an indivisible bond of fellowship, but with a wonderful daily communion he grows more and more into one body with us, until he becomes completely one with us. —*The Institutes* III.2.24

Christ, having been made ours, makes us sharers with him in the gifts with which he has been endowed. We do not, therefore, contemplate him outside ourselves from afar in order that his righteousness may be imputed to us but because we put on Christ and are engrafted into his body—in short, because he deigns to make us one with him. —*The Institutes* III.11.10

❹ On prayer.

. . . The essentials of prayer are set in the mind and heart, or rather that prayer itself is properly an emotion of the heart within, which is poured out and laid open before God, the searcher of hearts. —*The Institutes* III.20.29

True prayer ought to be nothing else but a pure affection of our heart as it is about to draw near to God . . . to pour out our prayers. —Calvin's *Catechism of* 1538

[Jesus] taught us to seek a retreat that would help us to descend into our heart with our whole thought and enter deeply within. He promises that God, whose temples our bodies ought to be, will be near to us in the affections of our hearts. —*The Institutes* III.20.29

HOW TO DISTINGUISH BETWEEN A JOB AND A CALLING

The Reformed idea of life and work embraces far more than a job or career. Reformed people are encouraged to discern their lives well in the hope that life and work mesh in a challenging, fulfilling, and God-glorifying package. Sometimes, though, people have no work or work at unpleasant jobs because of lack of options. The idea of "vocation" offers believers spiritual fulfillment and obedience to God whether they are pleased with their work or slaves to it.

Vocation comes from the Latin *vocatio*, meaning "a calling." The Roman Catholic Church still refers to the work and lives of priests and nuns as "vocations." This idea is fully compatible with a Reformed view of God calling and leading, but the Reformed view reaches beyond only full-time religious work. That is, God calls you to serve wherever you are (this is part of what John Calvin called the "sovereignty of God"). Thus Christ-believers go through a process of spiritual discernment to figure out what God is calling them to be and do—for a short time or a lifetime. Following a vocation also means that you don't necessarily go for the job that makes you the most money.

Be Aware

- You might discover that you are really good at several things.

- You might have the aptitude to be a doctor or a carpenter. Combining the two would produce an orthopedic surgeon—interesting work and beneficial to injured or careless people.

- You may be drawn toward a career or a compelling ability mysteriously but unmistakably—sometimes despite apparently closed doors. Maybe this is testing your mettle. An excerpt from Alexander McCall Smith's novel *Tears of the Giraffe* shows how a true vocation can surprise us. Mr. J.L.B. Matekoni has taken his new foster children to the garage where he works. He expects the boy to leap at engines, but the boy prefers drawing on the floor to picking up wrenches. Then Mr. Matekoni notices the boy's sister leaning eagerly forward in her wheelchair to watch him, her eyes bright with interest. "This girl . . . had the makings of a mechanic. He had never before seen it in a girl, but it was there" (p. 196).

HOW TO BE SAVED
(BY GRACE THROUGH FAITH
AND NOT BY GOOD WORKS)

Many religions are built on the idea that the more closely people follow religious rules or the more morally people behave, the better God will like them—and the better God likes them, the greater their chances of "getting into heaven."

While it is good to act morally and obey God's laws, such behavior will not save you. You don't need to be a follower of Jesus Christ to be a decent, upstanding person.

Christianity, on the other hand, says that out of pure love God was willing to sacrifice everything—even his only Son—to save you forever from sin, death, and all your false gods. Including you.

Since God has already done everything needed to secure your salvation through Jesus, you never have to do one single thing to earn God's favor, no matter how bad you are at following the rules. Whatever good we do is our thankful response to grace. Still, being saved takes some getting used to.

❶ **Get familiar with the word "grace."**
Grace means that God gives you all the good stuff—forgiveness, salvation, love, and life, with all its ups and downs—as totally free gifts. Look for situations in which you can use this word, and then use it liberally. You'll soon begin to see God's grace all around you.

❷ Practice letting go of things you love.
Staying focused on yourself can make it difficult to open up to a grace-filled world. But giving of yourself, your time, and your possessions can put you in a receptive, open frame of mind. This is important, as salvation cannot be "found" by looking for it; it is only revealed.

❸ Admit your limitations.
Without straying into despair or false modesty, make an honest confession to yourself about what you can and cannot do, what you are and what you are not. When you see yourself realistically you become more open to God's message of love, grace, and salvation.

❹ Accept your uniqueness.
In God's eyes, you were so valuable as to require the ultimate sacrifice of his Son, even before you spoke your first words. God will spend your whole life trying to convince you of this. When you accept that you are priceless to God beyond imagining, it becomes easier to understand why God chose to save you.

❺ Spend time in worship and prayer to the living God.
While only God grants the faith that saves, the church gives many opportunities to meet God.

❻ Avoid the temptation to "do."
The "old Adam" or "old Eve" in you—the sinner in you—always wants to be in charge over God. He or she will tell you that God's grace is too good to be true and that you must "do" something to earn or justify it. Simply remind your old self that you were baptized into Jesus Christ and have all the grace you need.

Be Aware

- The apostle Paul's summary of the gospel goes like this: "For by grace you have been saved through faith, and this is not your own doing; it is the gift of God— not the result of works, so that no one may boast" (Ephesians 2:8-9).

- This viewpoint about God's grace is unpopular, even among many Christians, as it was when Martin Luther and the reformers reminded the church of it almost 500 years ago. Be aware that once you adopt it you may come under fire and be tempted to lapse back into the old way.

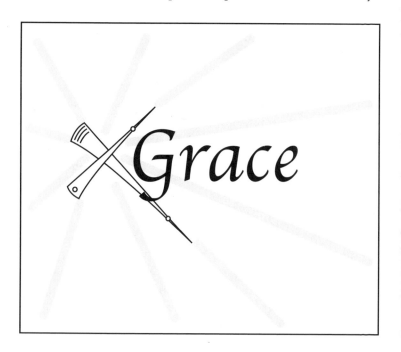

HOW TO REFORM THE CHURCH WHEN IT STRAYS FROM THE GOSPEL

When Martin Luther nailed his Ninety-five Theses to the church door in 1517, he took a stand against the corruption he saw in the church—false gospels, immoral leaders, and bad theology—and launched the Reformation.

From then on, by hanging on to his belief that only the free gift of faith in Christ could save him—and that the institutional church could not—Luther took a stand for an idea that survives today: *Ecclesia semper reformanda est* ("The church is always reforming"). To stay faithful to the gospel, the church still depends on all its members to call it back, not to their own personal visions, but to Jesus' vision.

❶ Know your stuff.
You can't call the church back to the gospel if you don't learn for yourself what the gospel is—your dislike of a certain practice is not by itself a guarantee that the church has gone off the rails. Read your Bible regularly. Join a small group Bible study or take an adult education class in your church on Bible books or themes. Spend time talking with good theologians, pastors, and church elders.

❷ Trust your conscience, but equip it first with good information.
To defy corrupt church authorities, Luther had to draw strength from even more powerful sources, namely his faith in God and his conscience. "It is neither safe nor right," he said, "to go against conscience."

❸ **Double-check and triple-check your motivations. Are you fighting on behalf of the gospel or for your own personal agenda?**
Knowing the difference between the two matters.
Some things may be worthy social causes that deserve your time and attention, but they may not be the gospel.

❹ **Speak out. Act.**
It isn't enough just to take a stand or hold an opinion. Once you're sure you're doing it for the right reasons, find an effective way to make change happen. Luther nailed the Ninety-five Theses in a public place (a common way to speak to the public in his day) and later used the printing press to spread his opinions to the widest possible audience. He put himself in the line of fire. In Strasbourg and Geneva John Calvin often advocated persistently for his points before hostile government officials. He didn't always win, but he always was very well prepared.

❺ **Prepare to defend yourself and your message of reform from attack.**
People tend to dislike reform—and institutions like it even less. While the church calls us to model the love of Christ and live by his teachings, sometimes the church and its leaders respond to reformers with a "kill the messenger" attitude.

❻ **Keep steady, be patient, and listen to wise counsel.**
The Reformation took decades to take root. During that time, the reformers battled church authorities. They also debated with each other about the best way to bring the gospel to a new age and restore the church to its real purpose.

Be Aware

- Not all efforts at reforming the church succeed. Refer to "How to Avoid Getting Burned at the Stake" (p. 64) for more information.

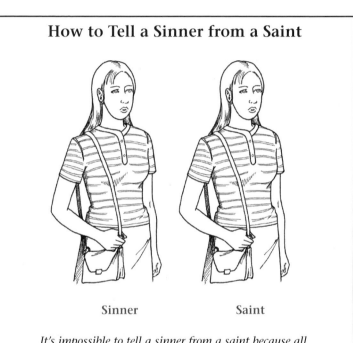

How to Tell a Sinner from a Saint

Sinner   Saint

It's impossible to tell a sinner from a saint because all Christ-believers are fully both. The church is filled with them.

HOW TO UNDERSTAND THE TRINITY AS ONE GOD IN THREE PERSONS

The Trinity is a mystery. Even great theologians don't completely understand, and some scholars spend their whole lives studying it. After 2,000 years, Christians still believe in this mystery because it gives life and shape to everything in our lives—our relationships, our faith, and especially our worship. Essentially the Trinity declares that God is an eternal community of love.

❶ **Get to know the three trinitarian creeds: the Nicene Creed, the Athanasian Creed, and the Apostles' Creed. Consider memorizing each one (one is pretty long).**
These three creeds were written during different times of crisis when heresies threatened the church's unity and clear statements about what Christians believed were needed. While different from each other, they each teach a lot about the three-personed God.

❷ **Spend time in the community of faith.**
Go to worship, fellowship, Bible study, Sunday school, and anything else that regularly keeps you in the company of other Christians.

❸ **Seek out God's Word and the means of grace.**
The Trinity is revealed in reading the Bible, preaching, the sacraments, the forgiveness of sins, the community of believers, and within anything else where Jesus, the living Word, is active.

Be Aware

- Some people use handy metaphors to begin to get a handle on the doctrine of the Trinity. For example, water takes three major forms: liquid, solid, and gas. Yet it remains one substance. Such metaphors are very useful to a point, but ultimately they must give way to the divine mystery that remains.

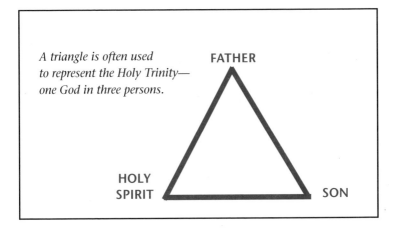

A triangle is often used to represent the Holy Trinity—one God in three persons.

FATHER

HOLY
SPIRIT

SON

BIBLE STUFF

Written down by many people over hundreds of years, the Bible is more like a portable bookshelf than one book by itself. And because the Bible is God's Word, people often feel overwhelmed when they try to read it.

This section includes:

- Helpful information about when, where, and why people wrote the 66 books within the Bible. (It didn't all come together at once.)

- Tips for reading and understanding the Bible— how it's organized and what it says.

- Some of the most mystifying, hair-raising, and just plain off-the-wall stories in the Bible.

COMMON ENGLISH TRANSLATIONS OF THE BIBLE

Translation Released	Grade Level*	Place in the Theological Spectrum	Year	Special Features
King James Version	12.0	Church of England, conservative and evangelical	1611	Poetic style using Elizabethan English. Most widely used translation for centuries.
New American Standard Bible	11.0	Conservative and evangelical	1971; updated, 1995	Revision of the 1901 American Standard Version into contemporary language.
New Revised Standard Version	8.1	Mainline and interconfessional	1989	Updated version of the Revised Standard Version.
New King James Version	8.0	Multidenominational, transdenominational, conservative, and evangelical	1982	Updates the King James text into contemporary language.
New International Version	7.8	Multidenominational, transdenominational, conservative, and evangelical	1978; revised, 1984	Popular modern-language version. Attempts to balance literal and dynamic translation methods.
Today's New International Version (TNIV)	7.8	Cross-denominational/ multidenominational, conservative and evangelical	2005	Newly-revised NIV using "gender accurate" language where appropriate according to the original texts.
				Noted for its freshness of language

Version	Grade level*	Tradition	Date	Description
New American Bible	6.6	Roman Catholic	1970; revised NT, 1986; revised Psalms, 1991	the Roman Catholic Church in the United States.
New Living Translation	6.4	Evangelical	1996	A meaning-for-meaning translation. Successor to the Living Bible.
New Century Version	5.6	Conservative and evangelical	1988; revised, 1991	Follows the *Living Word Vocabulary*.
Contemporary English Version	5.4	Conservative, evangelical, mainline	1995	Easy-to-read English for new Bible readers.
The Message	4.8, from NT samples	Evangelical	2002	An expressive paraphrase of the Bible.

*The grade level on which the text is written, using Dale-chall, Fry, Raygor, and Spache Formulas.

Bible classifications

Apocrypha Bible: Contains certain books that Protestants don't consider canonical. Most of these OT books are accepted by the Roman Catholic Church.

Children's Bible: Includes illustrations and other study aids that are especially helpful for children.

Concordance Bible: Lists places in the Bible where key words are found.

Red Letter Bible: The words spoken by Christ appear in red.

Reference Bible: Pages include references to other Bible passages on the same subject.

Self-Pronouncing Bible: Diacritical marks (as in a dictionary) appear above difficult names and words to help with the pronunciation.

Text Bible: Contains text without footnotes or column references. May include maps, illustrations, and other helpful material.

60 ESSENTIAL BIBLE STORIES

	Story	Bible Text	Key Verse
1.	Creation	Genesis 1-2	Genesis 1:27
2.	The Human Condition	Genesis 3-4	Genesis 3:5
3.	The Flood and the First Covenant	Genesis 6-9	Genesis 9:8
4.	The Tower of Babel and Abraham and Sarah	Genesis 11-12	Genesis 12:1
5.	Sarah, Hagar, and Abraham	Genesis 12-25	Genesis 17:19
6.	Isaac and Rebecca	Genesis 22-25	Genesis 24:67
7.	Jacob and Esau	Genesis 25-36	Genesis 28:15
8.	Joseph and God's Hidden Ways	Genesis 37-50	Genesis 50:20
9.	Moses and Pharaoh	Exodus 1-15	Exodus 2:23
10.	The Ten Commandments	Exodus 20	Exodus 20:2
11.	From the Wilderness into the Promised Land	Exodus 16-18; Deuteronomy 1-6; Joshua 1-3, 24	Deuteronomy 6:4
12.	Judges	Book of Judges	Judges 21:25
13.	Ruth	Book of Ruth	Ruth 4:14
14.	Samuel and Saul	1 Samuel 1-11	1 Samuel 3:1
15.	King David	multiple OT books	1 Samuel 8:6
16.	David, Nathan, and What Is a Prophet?	2 Samuel 11-12	2 Samuel 7:12
17.	Solomon	1 Kings 1-11	1 Kings 6:12
18.	Split of the Nation of Israel	1 Kings 11ff	1 Kings 12:16
19.	Northern Kingdom, Its Prophets and Fate	1 Kings—2 Kings 17	Amos 5:21
20.	Southern Kingdom, Its Prophets and Fate (Part 1)	multiple OT books	Isaiah 5:7

60 ESSENTIAL BIBLE STORIES

	Story	Bible Text	Key Verse
21.	Southern Kingdom, Its Prophets and Fate (Part 2)	multiple OT books	Jeremiah 31:31
22.	The Exile	Isaiah 40-55; Ezekiel	Isaiah 40:10
23.	Return from Exile	multiple OT books	Ezra 1:1
24.	Ezra and Nehemiah	Books of Ezra and Nehemiah	Ezra 3:10
25.	Esther	Book of Esther	Esther 4:14
26.	Job	Book of Job	Job 1:1
27.	Daniel	Book of Daniel	Daniel 3:17
28.	Psalms of Praise and Trust	Psalms 8, 30, 100, 113, 121	Psalm 121:1
29.	Psalms for Help	various psalms	Psalm 22:1
30.	Wisdom	Job, Proverbs, Ecclesiastes	Proverbs 1:7
31.	The Annunciation	Luke 1:26-56	Luke 1:31-33
32.	Magi	Matthew 2:1-12	Matthew 2:2-3
33.	Birth of Jesus	Luke 2:1-20	Luke 2:10-11
34.	Simeon	Luke 2:25-35	Luke 2:30-32
35.	Wilderness Temptations	Matthew 4:1-11; Mark 1:12-13; Luke 4:1-13	Luke 4:12-13
36.	Jesus' Nazareth Sermon	Matthew 13:54-58; Mark 6:1-6: Luke 4:16-30	Luke 4:18-19, 21
37.	Jesus Calls the First Disciples	Matthew 4:18-22; Mark 1:16-20; Luke 5:1-11	Luke 5:9-10
38.	Beatitudes	Matthew 5:3-12	Luke 6:20-26
39.	Feeding of the 5,000	Matthew 14:13-21; Mark 6:30-44; Luke 9:10-17; John 6:1-14	Luke 9:16-17
40.	The Transfiguration	Matthew 17:1-8; Mark 9:2-8: Luke 9:28-36	Luke 9:34-35

60 ESSENTIAL BIBLE STORIES

Story	Bible Text	Key Verse
41. Sending of the Seventy	Matthew 8:19-22; Luke 10:1-16	Luke 10:8, 16
42. Good Samaritan	Luke 10:25-37	Luke 10:27-28
43. Healing the Bent-Over Woman	Luke 13:10-17	Luke 13:10
44. Parables of Lost and Found	Luke 15:1-32	Luke 15:31-32
45. Rich Man and Lazarus	Luke 16:19-31	Luke 16:29-31
46. Zacchaeus	Luke 19:1-11	Luke 19:9
47. Sheep and Goats	Matthew 25:31-46	Matthew 25:40
48. Parable of the Vineyard	Matthew 21:33-46; Mark 12:1-12; Luke 20:9-19; (Isaiah 5:1-7)	Luke 20:14-16
49. The Last Supper	Matthew 26:20-29; Mark 14:12-16: Luke 22:14-38	Luke 22:19-20, 27
50. Crucifixion	Matthew 27; Mark 15; Luke 23; John 19	Luke 23:42-43, 46
51. Road to Emmaus	Luke 24	Luke 24:30-31
52. Pentecost	Acts 2:1-21	Acts 2:17-18
53. Healing the Lame Man	Acts 3-4	Acts 4:19
54. Baptism of the Ethiopian	Acts 8:26-39	Acts 8:35-37
55. Call of Saul	Acts 7:58—8:1, 9:1-30	Acts 9:15-16
56. Peter and Cornelius	Acts 10	Acts 10:34-35
57. Philippians Humility	Philippians 2:1-13	Philippians 2:12-13
58. Love Hymn	1 Corinthians 13	1 Corinthians 13:4-7
59. Resurrection	1 Corinthians 15	1 Corinthians 15:51-55
60. New Heavens and Earth	Revelation 21-22	Revelation 21:1

HOW TO READ THE BIBLE

The Bible is a collection of 66 separate books gathered
together over hundreds of years and thousands of miles.
Divided into the Old Testament (Hebrew language) and the
New Testament (Greek language), these writings have many
authors and take many forms. The Bible includes histories,
stories, prophecies, poetry, songs, teachings, and laws, to
name a few. Christians believe the Bible is the history of
God's relationship with humankind and a powerful way
that God speaks to people.

❶ Determine your purpose for reading.
Clarify in your own mind what you hope to gain. Your
motivation should be well-intentioned, such as to seek
information, to gain a deeper understanding of God and
yourself, or to enrich your faith. Pray for insight before
every reading time.

❷ Resolve to read daily.
Commit to a daily regimen of Bible reading. Make it part
of your routine until it becomes a habit.

*Commit to reading
the Bible daily.*

❸ Master the mechanics.

- Memorize the books of the Bible in order. There are catchy, simple songs that make this simple and that you'll remember all your life.

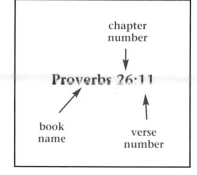

- Familiarize yourself with the introductory material. Many Bible translations include helpful information at the front of the Bible and at the beginning of each book.

- The books are broken down into chapters and verses. Locate the beginning of a book by using the Bible's table of contents. Follow the numerical chapter numbers; these are usually in large type. Verses are likewise numbered in order within each chapter. Simply run your finger down the page until you locate the verse number you're looking for.

- If your Bible contains maps (usually in the back), consult them when cities, mountains, or seas are mentioned in your reading.

❹ Befriend the written text.
Read with a pen or pencil in hand and underline passages of interest. Look up unfamiliar words in a dictionary. Write notes in the margins. The Bible was written to be read and used, not worshiped.

❺ Practice reading from the Bible out loud.

HOW TO MEMORIZE A BIBLE VERSE

Memorizing Scripture is an ancient faith practice. Its value is often mentioned by people who have, in crisis situations, remembered comforting or reassuring passages, sometimes decades after first memorizing them. There are three common methods of memorization.

Method 1: Memorize with Music

Choose a verse that is special for you. It is more difficult to remember something that doesn't make sense to you or that lacks meaning.

❶ Choose a familiar tune.
Pick something catchy and repetitious.

❷ Add the words from the Bible verse to your tune.
Mix up the words a bit, if necessary. Memorizing a verse "word for word" isn't always as important as learning the message of the verse.

❸ Mark the verse in your Bible.
This will help you find it again later on. Consider highlighting or underlining it.

❹ Make the words rhyme, if possible.

Method 2: The Three S's— "See it, Say it, Script it"

This method works on the principle of multisensory reinforcement. The brain creates many more neural pathways to a memory through sight, speech, and manipulation (writing) than just one of these, so recall is quicker and easier.

❶ Write the verse on index cards in large print. Post the cards in places you regularly look, such as the refrigerator door or bathroom mirror.

❷ Say the verse out loud. Repeat the verse ten times to yourself every time you notice one of your index cards.

❸ Write the verse down.

❹ Try saying and writing the verse at the same time. Repeat.

Method 3: Old-Fashioned Memorization

Attempt this method only if you consider yourself to be "old school" or if the other methods fail.

Write the verse out longhand several dozen times.

❶ Write the verse out by hand on paper.
A whiteboard can work extremely well also. Consider
writing it as many as 100 times. Repeat this process until
you can recite the verse flawlessly.

❷ Don't get up until you've memorized the verse.
Open your Bible to the appropriate verse, sit down in
front of it, and don't get up, eat, sleep, or use the bathroom until you can recite it flawlessly.

❸ Enlist a family member or friend to help you.
Have him or her read along with you and prompt you
when you get stuck.

THE TOP TEN BIBLE VILLAINS

❶ Satan
The Evil One is known by many names in the Bible and appears many places, but the devil's purpose is always the same: To disrupt and confuse people so they turn from God and seek to become their own gods. This Bible villain is still active today.

❷ The Serpent
In Eden, the serpent succeeded in tempting Eve to eat from the tree of the knowledge of good and evil (Genesis 3:1-7). As a result, sin entered creation. If it weren't for the serpent, would we all still be walking around naked, eating fresh fruit, and living forever?

❸ Pharaoh (probably Seti I or Rameses II)
The notorious Pharaoh from the book of Exodus enslaved the Israelites. Moses eventually begged him to "Let my people go," but Pharaoh hardened his heart and refused. Ten nasty plagues later, Pharaoh relented, but then changed his mind again. In the end, with the Egyptian army at the bottom of the sea, God miraculously gave the Israelites their freedom.

❹ Goliath
"The Philistine of Gath," who stood six cubits in height (about nine feet tall), was sent to fight David, still a downy-cheeked youth. Goliath was a fighting champion known for killing people, but David drilled Goliath in the head with a rock from his sling and gave God the glory (1 Samuel 17).

❺ Jezebel

King Ahab of Judah's wife and a follower of the false god Baal, Jezebel led her husband away from God and tried to kill off the prophets of the Lord. Elijah the prophet, however, was on the scene. He shamed Jezebel's false prophets and killed them (1 Kings 18:40).

❻ King Herod

Afraid of any potential threat to his power, on hearing about the Messiah's birth in Bethlehem, Herod sent the Wise Men to pinpoint his location. Awestruck by the Savior, the Wise Men went home by a different route and avoided Herod. In a rage, he ordered the murder of every child two years of age or younger in the vicinity of Bethlehem. The baby Jesus escaped with his parents to Egypt (Matthew 2:14-15).

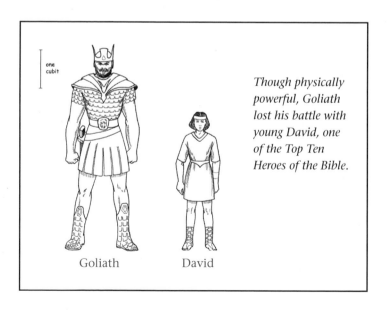

one cubit

Though physically powerful, Goliath lost his battle with young David, one of the Top Ten Heroes of the Bible.

Goliath   David

❼ The Pharisees, Sadducees, and Scribes

They dogged Jesus throughout his ministry, alternately challenging his authority and being awed by his power. It was their leadership, with the consent and blessing of the people and the Roman government, that brought Jesus to trial and execution.

❽ Judas

One of Jesus' original disciples, Judas earned thirty pieces of silver by betraying his Lord to the authorities. He accomplished this by leading the soldiers into the garden of Gethsemane where he revealed Jesus with a kiss (Matthew 26-27).

❾ Pontius Pilate

This Roman governor chose to preserve his own bloated status by giving the people what they wanted: Jesus' crucifixion. He washed his hands to signify self-absolution, but bloodied them instead.

❿ God's People

They whine, they sin, they turn their backs on God over and over again. When given freedom, they blow it. When preached repentance by God's prophets, they stone them. When offered a Savior, they kill him. In the end, it must be admitted, God's people—us!—don't really shine. Only by God's grace and the gift of faith in Jesus Christ do we have hope.

THE TOP TEN BIBLE HEROES

The Bible is filled with examples of people who, against all odds, follow God no matter the outcome. These are heroes of faith. (See Hebrews 11 for more.)

❶ Noah

In the face of ridicule from others, Noah trusted God when God chose him to build an ark to save a remnant of humanity from destruction.

❷ Abraham and Sarah

Abraham and Sarah answered God's call to leave their home and travel to a strange land. The nation of Israel began years later, when Sarah, then a very old woman, gave birth to Isaac.

Noah trusted God, even though others made fun of him. By following God's instructions and building a great ark, Noah and his family survived the flood (Genesis 6–10).

❸ Moses
Moses challenged the Egyptian king ("Pharaoh") to deliver God's people from bondage. He led a rebellious and contrary people for forty years through the wilderness and gave them God's law.

❹ Rahab
A prostitute who helped Israel conquer the Promised Land, Rahab was the great-grandmother of King David, and thus part of the family of Jesus himself.

❺ David
Great King David, the youngest member of his family, defeated great enemies, turning Israel into a world power. He wrote poems and songs (psalms), led armies, and confessed his sins to the Lord.

❻ Mary and Joseph
These humble peasants responded to God's call to be the earthly parents of Jesus Christ, the Messiah, although the call came through a pregnancy that was not the result of marriage.

❼ The Canaanite Woman
Desperate for her daughter's health, the Canaanite woman challenged Jesus regarding race by claiming God's love for all people (Matthew 15:21-28). Because of this, Jesus praised her faith.

❽ Peter
Peter was quick to speak but slow to think. At Jesus' trial, Peter denied ever having known him. But in the power of forgiveness and through Christ's appointment, Peter became a leader in the early church.

⑨ Saul/Paul

Originally an enemy and persecutor of Christians, Paul experienced a powerful vision of Jesus, was converted, and became the greatest missionary the church has ever known.

⑩ Phoebe

A contemporary of Paul's, Phoebe is believed to have delivered the book of Romans after traveling some 800 miles from Cenchrea near Corinth to Rome. A wealthy woman, she used her influence to travel, protect other believers, and to host worship services in her home.

Phoebe is believed to have delivered the book of Romans after traveling 800 miles.

THE THREE MOST REBELLIOUS THINGS JESUS DID

❶ The prophet returned to his hometown (Luke 4:14-27).

Jesus returned to Nazareth, where he was raised and was invited to read Scripture and preach. First, he insisted that the scriptures he read were not just comforting promises of a distant future, but that they were about him, a local boy, anointed by God. Second, he insisted God would bless foreigners with those same promises through him. These statements amounted to the unpardonable crime of blasphemy!

❷ The rebel thumbed his nose at the authorities (John 11:55-12:11).

Jesus had become an outlaw, hunted by the religious authorities who wanted to kill him. After Jesus raised Lazarus from the dead, Mary, Martha, and Lazarus threw a thank-you party for Jesus in Bethany, right outside Jerusalem, the authorities' stronghold. In spite of the threats to his life, Jesus went to the party. This was not just rebellion but a demonstration of how much Jesus loved his friends.

❸ The king rode a royal procession right under Caesar's nose (Matthew 21:1-17; Mark 11:1-10; Luke 19:28-38; John 12:12-19).

Jesus entered Jerusalem during a great festival, in full view of adoring crowds, as a king come home to rule. Riding the colt, heralded by the people with cloaks and branches, accompanied by the royal anthem (Psalm 118), he rode in to claim Jerusalem for God and himself as God's anointed. The Roman overlords and the Jewish leaders watched this seditious act and prepared for a crucifixion.

THE SEVEN FUNNIEST BIBLE STORIES

Humor isn't scarce in the Bible; you just have to look for it. For example, God tells Abraham (100 years old) and Sarah (in her 90s) they'll soon have a son. Understandably, they laugh. Later, they have a son named Isaac, which means "he [or she!] laughs." Bible humor is also ironic, gross, and sometimes just plain bizarre.

❶ **Gideon's dog-men (Judges 6:11-7:23).**
God chooses Gideon to lead an army against the Midianites. Gideon gathers an army of 32,000 men, but this is too many. God tells Gideon to make all the men drink from a stream, and then selects only the 300 men who lap water like dogs.

❷ **David ambushes Saul in a cave while he's "busy" (1 Samuel 24:2-7).**
While pursuing David cross-country to engage him in battle, Saul goes into a cave to "relieve himself" (move his bowels). Unbeknownst to Saul, David and his men are already hiding in the very same cave. While Saul's doing his business, David sneaks up and cuts off a corner of Saul's cloak with a knife. Outside afterward, David shows King Saul the piece of cloth to prove he could have killed him "on the throne."

❸ **King David does the goofy (2 Samuel 12-23).**
David is so excited about bringing the Ark of the Covenant to Jerusalem that he dances before God and all the people dressed only in a linen ephod, apron-like underwear that covered only the front of his body.

Balaam's donkey

❹ Baalam's donkey (Numbers 22:21-36)

When Moab's King Balak hired a well-known fortune teller named Balaam to curse the Israelites, God's angel stood in Balaam's way. His donkey saw the angel, though Balaam himself did not. After he beat the donkey three times, the animal actually asked Balaam why he was doing that. As if that's not funny enough, Balaam even answered. After that, Balaam blessed the Israelites instead of cursing them as his boss had demanded. Makes you wonder if King Balak ever paid Balaam's fee for services.

❺ Gerasene demoniac (Mark 5:1-20).

A man is possessed by so many demons that chains cannot hold him. Jesus exorcises the demons and sends them into a herd of 2,000 pigs, which then run over the edge of a cliff and drown in the sea. The herders, now 2,000 pigs poorer, get miffed and ask Jesus to leave. If the owners were Jewish, why did they admit to even owning pigs?

⑥ Disciples and loaves of bread (Mark 8:14-21).
The disciples were there when Jesus fed 5,000 people
with just five loaves of bread and two fish. They also saw
him feed 4,000 people with seven loaves. Later, in a boat,
the disciples fret to an exasperated Jesus because they
have only one loaf for thirteen people.

⑦ Peter can't swim (Matthew 14:22-33).
Blundering Peter sees Jesus walking on the water and
wants to join him. But when he looks down at the water,
Peter panics and starts to sink. In Greek, the name Peter
means "rock," which he most resembled when he sank.

Peter, "the rock," sank when he looked to himself instead of to Jesus. Jesus later described Peter as a Rock of the church (Matthew 16:18).

THE FIVE GROSSEST BIBLE STORIES

❶ Eglon and Ehud (Judges 3:12-30).
Before kings ruled Israel, judges led the people. At that time, a king named Eglon conquered Israel and demanded money. A left-handed man named Ehud was from the tribe of Benjamin (meaning "son of my right hand"!) brought the payment to Eglon while he was perched on his "throne" (maybe meaning "toilet"). Along with the money, Ehud handed over a little something extra—his sword, which he buried so far in Eglon's belly that the sword disappeared and, as the Bible says, "the dirt came out" (v. 22).

❷ Job's sores (Job 2:1-10).
Job lived a righteous life yet he suffered anyway. He had oozing sores from the bald spot on top of his head clear down to the soft spot on the bottom of his foot. Job used a broken piece of pottery to scrape away the pus that leaked from his sores.

❸ The naked prophet (Isaiah 20).
God's prophets went to great lengths to get God's message across to the people. Isaiah was no exception. God's people planned a war, but God gave it the thumbs down. Isaiah marched around Jerusalem naked *for three years* as a sign of what would happen if the people went to war.

❹ The almost-naked prophet (Jeremiah 13:1-11).
God sent Jeremiah to announce that God could no longer be proud of the people. To make the point, Jeremiah bought a new pair of underclothes, wore them every day

Filthy
underwear

Jeremiah strapped on some filthy underwear to show God could no longer be proud of the people.

without washing them, then buried them in the wet river sand. Later, he dug them up, strapped them on, and shouted that this is what has happened to the people who were God's pride!

❺ **Spilling your guts (Matthew 27:1-8; Acts 1:16-19).** Judas betrayed Jesus and sold him out for thirty pieces of silver. Guilt-stricken, Judas hanged himself. When he fell or was cut down, his belly burst, and his intestines spilled out onto the ground.

FIVE FACTS ABOUT LIFE
IN OLD TESTAMENT TIMES

❶ Almost everyone wore sandals.
They were called "sandals" because people walked on sand much of the time. (If you believe this, we have a bridge for sale in Brooklyn at a good price.)

❷ There were no newspapers.
People got news by hearing it from other people. Spreading important news was like a giant game of "telephone."

❸ It was dark.
Homes, often tents, were typically lit at night by an oil lamp, if at all.

❹ You had to fetch your water, which was scarce.
Rich folks had servants to carry it for them, but most people had to carry household water in jugs or leather bags, usually some distance, from a river or well.

❺ Life expectancy was short.
Despite some long-lived exceptions mentioned in Genesis, such as Abraham (175 years) and Methuselah (969 years), few people lived past 50.

Sandals were made for walking on sand.

TEN IMPORTANT THINGS THAT HAPPENED BETWEEN THE OLD AND NEW TESTAMENTS

The period of time described in the Old Testament ended about 400 years before Jesus' birth. The people of God kept living, believing, struggling, and writing during that period. Here are some important events that took place between the Testaments.

❶ **The Hebrew nation dissolved.**
In 587 B.C., the Babylonians destroyed Jerusalem and Solomon's temple and took the people into exile. Judah was never again an independent kingdom.

❷ **The people scattered.**
After the exile to Babylon ended, the people of Judah moved to many different places. Some later returned but many never did. Some lived in Babylon, some lived in Egypt, and some just scattered elsewhere.

❸ **A religion replaced a nation.**
As a result of items 1 and 2, the people's religion changed. They no longer had a state or national religion (Judean religion). Instead, they had a freestanding faith called Judaism.

❹ **The Aramaic language became popular.**
Because Aramaic was the international language of the Persian Empire, many Jews quit speaking Hebrew and spoke Aramaic instead. This is why Jesus spoke Aramaic.

❺ Alexander the Great conquered the world.
Around 330 B.C., Alexander the Great conquered the
Mediterranean and Mesopotamian world. As a result,
Greek became the everyday language of business and
trade in the region. This is why the New Testament was
written in Greek.

❻ The hammer dropped.
Around 170 B.C., the Seleucid emperor outlawed
circumcision and the Sabbath, and defiled the temple.
A family of Jews called the Maccabees (which means
"hammer") led a revolt.

❼ The Hebrew Scriptures were finished.
During this time, the individual books that make up
what we call the Old Testament were finished. Several
other religious books written at this time (mostly in
Greek) aren't in the Protestant Bible but are part of the
Apocrypha.

**❽ The Sadducees, Pharisees, Essenes, Samaritans,
Zealots, and other groups of people sprouted up.**
Different schools of thought developed within Judaism.
Their biggest religious disagreements were over the idea
that God's people would be resurrected to eternal life.
Politically the Pharisees were fierce patriots and often
rebellious against Rome, while the Sadducees tended to
be more agreeable with Rome. These two political rivals
came together in their opposition to Jesus.

❾ God seemed to have forgotten the promise.
God promised King David that one of his descendants
would always be king in Jerusalem. But after the Baby-
lonian exile, there were no kings in Jerusalem. People
wondered what had happened to God's promise.

⑩ The Roman Empire expanded.

In 63 B.C., the Roman Empire conquered Palestine, having already conquered pretty much everyone else in the region. This is why the Roman Empire ruled the area during the time of Jesus and the New Testament.

FIVE FACTS ABOUT LIFE IN NEW TESTAMENT TIMES

❶ Synagogues were not always buildings.
For worship, Jesus' people gathered in all kinds of places, often outdoors. "Church" was any gathering of people for worship.

❷ Houses were boxy.
Most houses had a flat roof with an outside staircase leading to it. Inhabitants would sleep on the roof during hot weather.

Houses in New Testament times were boxy.

❸ Every town had a marketplace.
Usually there was just one marketplace per town, but one could buy almost everything needed to live.

❹ People ate a lot of fish.
The most common fish in the Sea of Galilee were catfish and carp. Roasting over a charcoal fire was the most common method of cooking.

❺ Dogs were shunned.
The Jewish people in Jesus' day did not keep dogs as pets. Dogs were considered unclean because they ate garbage and animal carcasses.

THE FIVE BIGGEST MISCONCEPTIONS ABOUT THE BIBLE

❶ The Bible was written in a short period of time.
Christians believe that God inspired the Bible writers, the first of whom may have been Moses. God inspired people to write down important histories, traditions, songs, wise sayings, poetry, and prophetic words. All told—from the first recordings of the stories in Genesis to the last decisions about Revelation—the entire Bible formed over a period spanning anywhere from 800 to 1,400 years!

❷ One person wrote the Bible.
Unlike Islam's Koran, which was written by the prophet Muhammad, the books of the Bible are the handiwork of many people. Much of Scripture does not identify the human hand that wrote it.

❸ The entire Bible should be taken literally.
While many parts of the Bible are meant as descriptions of actual historical events, other parts are intended as *illustrations of God's truth*, such as Song of Solomon, the book of Revelation, and Jesus' parable of the good Samaritan. So when Jesus says, "If your right eye causes you to sin, tear it out and throw it away" (Matthew 5:29), please do not take the saying literally!

❹ People in Bible times were unenlightened.
During the 1,400 years it took to write the Bible, some of history's greatest thinkers lived and worked. Many of these philosophers, architects, mathematicians, orators,

theologians, historians, doctors, military tacticians, inventors, engineers, poets, and playwrights are still quoted today and their works are still in use.

⑤ The Bible is a single book.
The Bible is actually a collection of books, letters, and other writings—more like a library than a book. There are thirty-nine books in the Hebrew scriptures, what Christians call the "Old" Testament, and twenty-seven books (mostly letters) in the New Testament. There are seven books in the Apocrypha (books written between the Old and New Testaments), or "deuterocanonical" books. But this collection tells one *story* of God's salvation.

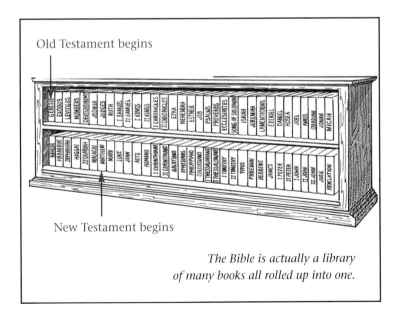

Old Testament begins

New Testament begins

The Bible is actually a library
of many books all rolled up into one.

JESUS' TWELVE APOSTLES (PLUS JUDAS AND PAUL)

While Jesus had many disciples (students and followers), the Bible focuses particularly on twelve who were closest to him. Tradition says that these twelve spread Jesus' message throughout the known world (Matthew 28:18-20). For this reason, they were known as *apostles*, a word that means "sent ones." Sometimes the disciples get a bum rap, because admittedly they did some dumb things—trying to chase children away from Jesus, arguing over who was the greatest (Mark 9:33 ff.). James and John's mother, Mrs. Zebedee, tried to cozy up to Jesus to secure top billing for her boys in the kingdom of heaven (Matthew 20:20ff.). And Peter denied Jesus three times after Jesus was arrested (John 18:15-18, 25-27).

Instead of dissing the disciples for their failures, keep in mind that they were learning and living under great stress, uncertainty, and persecution. Also appreciate what Episcopalian preacher Fleming Rutledge reminds us: "All these people gave their lives in order that you and I might know the Gospel of God's amazing grace in Jesus Christ." So thank God for those people.

❶ Andrew
A fisherman and the first disciple to follow Jesus, Andrew brought his brother, Simon Peter, to Jesus.

❷ Bartholomew
Also called Nathanael, tradition has it that he was martyred by being skinned alive.

❸ James the Elder
James, with John and Peter, was one of Jesus' closest disciples. Herod Agrippa killed James because of his faith, which made him a martyr (Acts 12:2).

❹ John
John (or one of his followers) is thought to be the author of the Gospel of John and three letters of John and Revelation. He probably died of natural causes in old age in exile on the island of Patmos in the Aegean Sea.

❺ Matthew
Matthew was a tax collector and, therefore, probably an outcast even among his own people. He is attributed with the authorship of the Gospel of Matthew. In Mark and Luke the same person is called Levi.

❻ Peter
Peter was a fisherman who was brought to faith by his brother Andrew. He was probably martyred in Rome by being crucified upside down.

❼ Philip
Philip, possibly a Greek, is responsible for bringing Bartholomew (Nathanael) to faith. He is thought to have died in a city called Phrygia.

❽ James the Less
James was called "the Less" so he wouldn't be confused with James, the brother of John, or Jesus' brother James.

❾ Simon
Simon is often called "the Zealot." Zealots were a political group in Jesus' day that favored the overthrow of the Roman government by force.

⑩ Jude

Jude may have worked with Simon the Zealot in Persia (Iran) where they were reportedly martyred on the same day.

⑪ Thomas

"Doubting" Thomas preached the message of Jesus in India.

⑫ Matthias

Matthias was chosen by lot to replace Judas. It is thought that he worked mostly in Ethiopia.

⑬ Judas Iscariot

Judas was the treasurer for Jesus' disciples and the one who betrayed Jesus for thirty pieces of silver. According to the Bible, Judas killed himself for his betrayal.

⑭ Paul

Paul is considered primarily responsible for bringing non-Jewish people to faith in Jesus. He traveled extensively throughout the whole Mediterranean Sea basin and wrote many letters to believers. Many of Paul's letters are included in the New Testament.

THE FIVE WEIRDEST LAWS IN THE OLD TESTAMENT

The Old Testament has many helpful, common sense laws, such as "You shall not kill," and, "You shall not steal." But there are a few others that need some explaining.

❶ The "ox" law.

"When an ox gores a man or a woman to death, the ox shall be stoned, and its flesh shall not be eaten; but the owner of the ox shall not be liable" (Exodus 21:28). Replace "ox" with "car" and the law makes more sense; it is about protecting others from reckless actions.

People living in biblical times were sometimes gored by oxen.

People who were gored by oxen— or victims of other crimes— had legal recourse.

❷ The "no kid boiling" law.
"You shall not boil a kid in its mother's milk" (Exodus 23:19b). By the way, a "kid" is a juvenile goat, not a little person!

❸ The "which bugs are legal to eat" law.
"All flying insects that walk upon all fours are detestable to you. There are some winged insects that walk on all fours that you may eat—those with jointed legs for hopping on the ground" (Leviticus 11:20-21). The law is unclear whether it is legal to eat the bug if you first pull off the legs. By the way, locusts were John the Baptist's main source of protein (Matthew 3:4).

❹ The "don't eat blood" law.
"No person among you shall eat blood" (Leviticus 17:12). Some laws make you wonder whether people in that time had any sense of taste. On the other hand, blood sausage is still popular with some people.

❺ The "pure cloth" law.
"You shall not wear clothes made of wool and linen woven together" (Deuteronomy 22:11). Polyester and spandex came along after Bible times.

THE TOP TEN BIBLE MIRACLES AND WHAT THEY MEAN

❶ Creation.
God created the universe and everything that is in it, and God continues to sustain and care for all he created.

❷ The Passover.
The Israelites were enslaved by Pharaoh, a ruler who believed the people belonged to him, not to God. In the last of ten plagues, God visited the homes and farms of all the Egyptians to kill the firstborn male (human and animal) in each one. God alone is Lord of all people, and no human can claim ultimate power over us.

❸ The Exodus.
God's people were fleeing Egypt when Pharaoh dispatched his army to force them back into slavery. The army trapped the people with their backs to a sea, but God parted the water and the people walked across to freedom while Pharaoh's soldiers were destroyed. God chose to free us from all forms of tyranny so we may use that freedom to serve God and each other.

❹ Manna.
After the people crossed the sea to freedom, they complained that they were going to starve to death. They even begged to return to Egypt. God sent *manna* which some have called "bread of heaven." *Manna* is a Hebrew word that means "What is it?" God cares for us even when we give up, pine for our slavery, and lose faith. God never abandons us.

❺ The Incarnation.
The immortal and infinite God became a human being, choosing to be born of a woman. God loved us enough to

become one of us in Jesus of Nazareth, forever bridging the
divide that had separated us from God. "Incarnation" comes
from the same Latin word as "carne" (Spanish for "meat"),
an astonishing fact that helps hammer home the extent to
which God humbled himself (see Philippians 2:5-11).

❻ Jesus healed a paralyzed man.
Some men brought a paralyzed friend to Jesus. Jesus said,
"Son, your sins are forgiven" (Mark 2:5). This shows that Jesus
has the power to forgive our sins—and he does so as a free gift.

❼ Jesus calmed the storm.
Jesus was asleep in a boat with his disciples when a great
storm came up and threatened to sink it. He said, "Peace!
Be still!" (Mark 4:39). Then the storm immediately
calmed. Jesus is Lord over even the powers of nature.

❽ The Resurrection.
People executed Jesus, but God raised him from the
dead on the third day. Through baptism, we share in
Jesus' death, so we will also share in eternal life with God
the Father, Son, and Holy Spirit. Christ conquered death.

❾ Pentecost.
Jesus ascended from the earth, but he did not leave the
church powerless or alone. On the fiftieth day after the
Jewish Passover (Pentecost means fiftieth), Jesus sent the
Holy Spirit to create the church and take up residence
among us. The Holy Spirit is present with us always.

❿ The Second Coming.
One day, Christ will come again and end all suffering.
This means that the final result of the epic battle between
good and evil is already assured. It is simply that evil has
not yet admitted defeat.

THE EXODUS

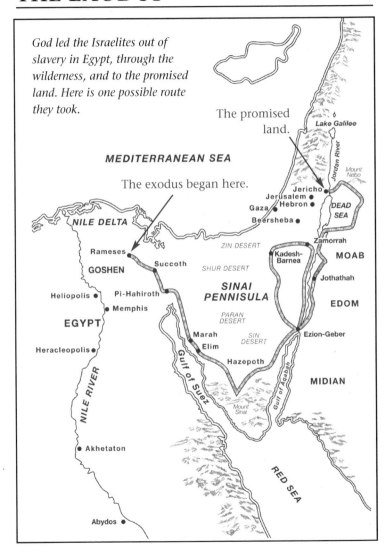

God led the Israelites out of slavery in Egypt, through the wilderness, and to the promised land. Here is one possible route they took.

The promised land.

The exodus began here.

MEDITERRANEAN SEA

Lake Galilee

Jordan River

Mount Nebo

Jericho
Jerusalem
Gaza Hebron
Beersheba

DEAD SEA

NILE DELTA

Rameses
GOSHEN Succoth

ZIN DESERT
SHUR DESERT

Kadesh-Barnea

Zamorrah

MOAB

Heliopolis
Memphis

Pi-Hahiroth

SINAI PENNISULA

PARAN DESERT

Jothathah

EDOM

EGYPT

Marah
Elim

SIN DESERT

Ezion-Geber

Heracleopolis

Hazepoth

MIDIAN

NILE RIVER

Gulf of Suez

Gulf of Aqabah

Mount Sinai

Akhetaton

RED SEA

Abydos

THE HOLY LAND—
OLD TESTAMENT TIMES

THE HOLY LAND—
NEW TESTAMENT TIMES

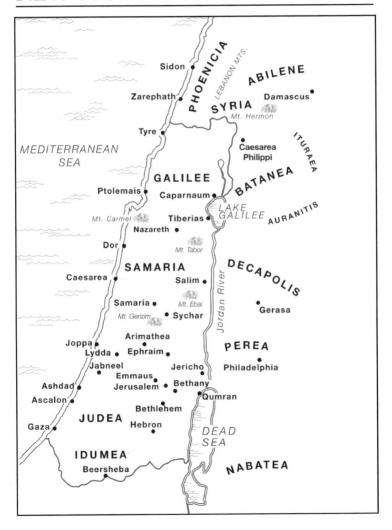

PAUL'S JOURNEYS

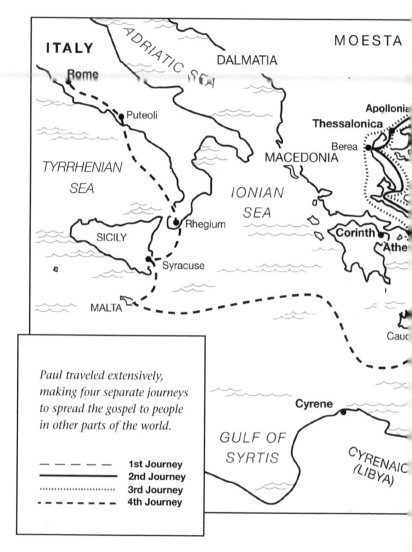

ITALY

ADRIATIC SEA

MOESTA

DALMATIA

Rome

Puteoli

Apollonia

Thessalonica

Berea

MACEDONIA

TYRRHENIAN SEA

IONIAN SEA

Corinth

Rhegium

Athe

SICILY

Syracuse

MALTA

Caud

Paul traveled extensively,
making four separate journeys
to spread the gospel to people
in other parts of the world.

Cyrene

GULF OF
SYRTIS

CYRENAIC
(LIBYA)

– – – – – 1st Journey
─────── 2nd Journey
.... 3rd Journey
– ‑ – ‑ – ‑ 4th Journey

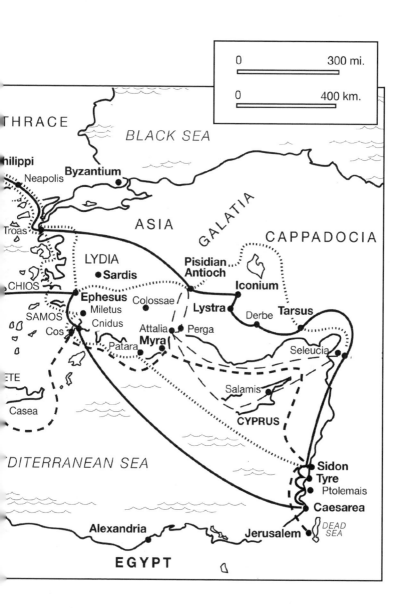

JERUSALEM IN JESUS' TIME

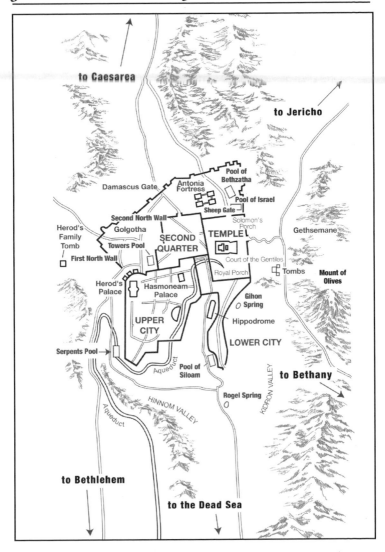

NOAH'S ARK

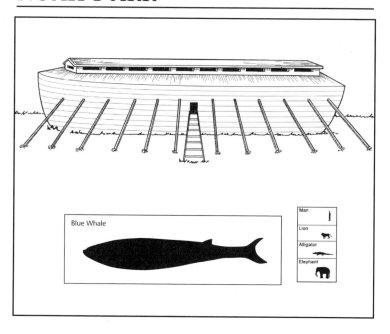

A cubit is equal to the length of a man's forearm from the elbow to the tip of the middle finger—approximately 18 inches or 45.7 centimeters. Noah's ark was 300 cubits long, 50 cubits wide, and 30 cubits tall (Genesis 6:15).

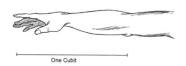

One Cubit

THE ARK OF THE COVENANT

God told the Israelites to place the stone tablets—the "covenant"—of the law into the Ark of the Covenant. The Israelites believed that God was invisibly enthroned above the vessel and went before them wherever they traveled.

The Ark of the Covenant was 2.5 cubits long and 1.5 cubits wide (Exodus 25:17).

Cherubim

Gold plating

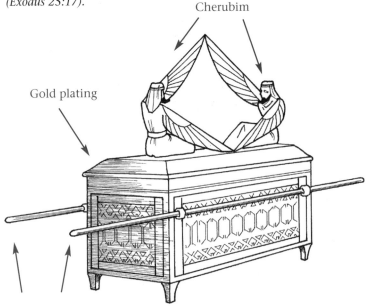

Carrying poles

Exodus 25:10-22

SOLOMON'S TEMPLE

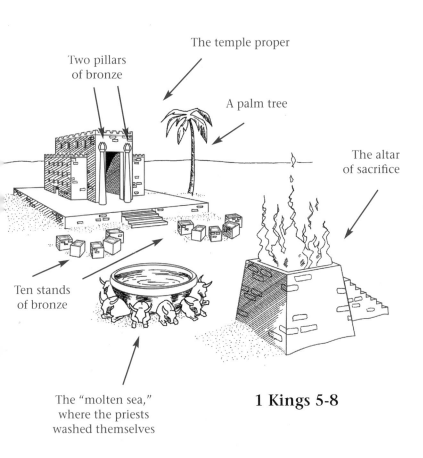

The temple proper

Two pillars
of bronze

A palm tree

The altar
of sacrifice

Ten stands
of bronze

The "molten sea,"
where the priests
washed themselves

1 Kings 5-8

THE ARMOR OF GOD

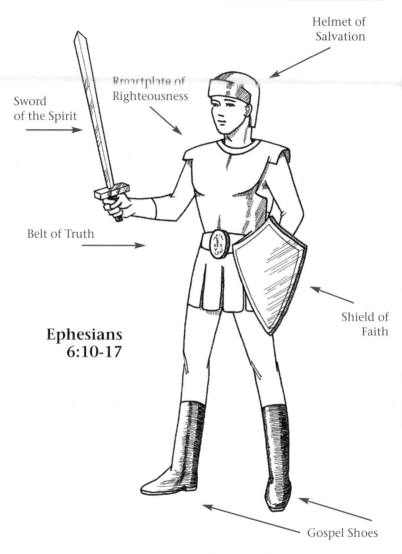

Helmet of
Salvation

Breastplate of
Righteousness

Sword
of the Spirit

Belt of Truth

Shield of
Faith

**Ephesians
6:10-17**

Gospel Shoes

THE PASSION AND CRUCIFIXION

Judas betrayed Jesus with a kiss, saying, "the one I will kiss is the man; arrest him" (Matthew 26:48).

Peter denied Jesus three times (Matthew 26:69-75).

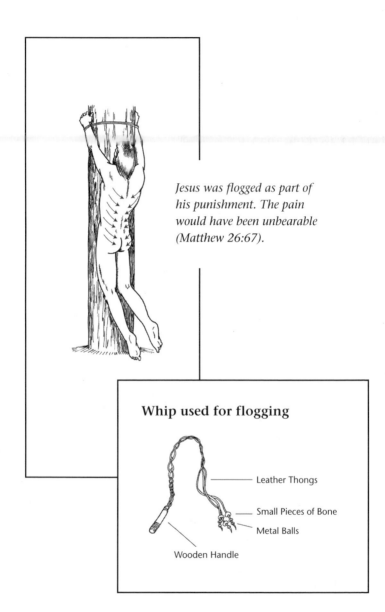

Jesus was flogged as part of his punishment. The pain would have been unbearable (Matthew 26:67).

Whip used for flogging

Leather Thongs

Small Pieces of Bone

Metal Balls

Wooden Handle

After being flogged, carrying the patibulum was nearly impossible for Jesus.

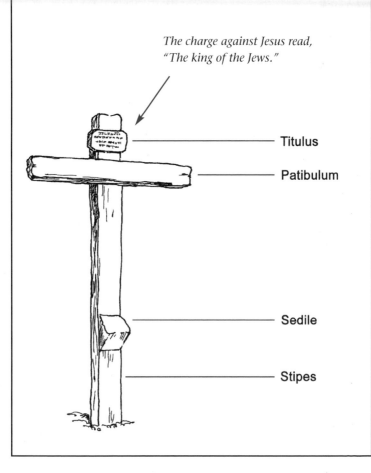

Crucifixion was so common in Jesus' time that the Romans had special names for the parts of the cross.

The charge against Jesus read, "The king of the Jews."

Titulus

Patibulum

Sedile

Stipes

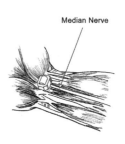

Median Nerve

Typical crucifixion involved being nailed to the cross through the wrists—an excruciatingly painful and humiliating punishment. Criminals and traitors were commonly executed by this method—think of lethal injection, hanging, or electrocution today. That's what Jesus physically suffered in your place.

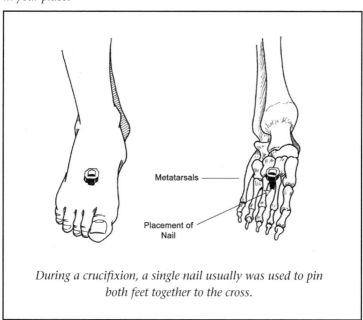

Metatarsals

Placement of Nail

During a crucifixion, a single nail usually was used to pin both feet together to the cross.

Eventually, the victim would be unable to lift himself to take a breath, and he would suffocate.

While the Romans broke the legs of the men who were crucified next to Jesus, they found that Jesus had already died. To make sure, they pierced his side with a spear, probably to puncture his heart (John 19:34).

Joseph of Arimathea and several women took Jesus down and carried him to the tomb (Matthew 27:57-61).

The miracle of resurrection took place three days later, when Jesus rose from the dead.

THE HEIDELBERG CATECHISM

A "catechism" is a progressive series of questions and answers. This format has long been used to teach youth and adults key biblical themes and theological doctrines. The Heidelberg Catechism was composed in Heidelberg, Germany, at the request of Elector Frederick III, who ruled the Palatinate in central Germany from 1559 to 1576. Zacharius Ursinus and Caspar Olevianus are considered coauthors of the catechism, though one may have had primary responsibility.

The "Heidelberger," as many refer to it, consists of 129 questions and answers organized into 52 sections called "Lord's Days." These are intended to be taught or preached in worship services on successive Sundays of the year. The Catechism is divided into three main themes: Sin (or misery), deliverance, and thankfulness. These themes are memorably expressed as "Guilt, Grace, and Gratitude" or "Sin, Salvation, and Service." The Catechism's questions and answers provide explanations and practical, personal applications of the Apostles' Creed, the Sacraments of baptism and the Lord's Supper, the Ten Commandments, and the Lord's Prayer.

One of the characteristics of the Heidelberg Catechism is its personal warmth. If often asks things like "How does . . . comfort you?"

After the Heidelberg Catechism was approved by the Synod of Dort in the Netherlands (1618-1619), it soon became the most widely used of the Reformed catechisms and confessions. It has been translated into many European, Asian, and African languages. The Christian Reformed Church's 1975 translation is the basis for the abridgement in this handbook. The entire catechism is available online at http://www.crcna.org/pages/heidelberg_main.cfm.

INTRODUCTION

Q&A 1 of Lord's Day 1 is probably the best-known and most memorized expression of Reformed doctrine:

1. Q. **What is your only comfort in life and in death?**
   A. That I am not my own,

   but belong—
      body and soul,
      in life and in death—
   to my faithful Savior Jesus Christ.

   He has fully paid for all my sins with his precious
   blood, and has set me free from the tyranny of
   the devil. He also watches over me in such a way
   that not a hair can fall from my head without the
   will of my Father in heaven: in fact, all things
   must work together for my salvation.

   Because I belong to him,
   Christ, by his Holy Spirit,
   assures me of eternal life
   and makes me wholeheartedly willing and ready
   from now on to live for him.

(Romans 8:1-17)

The second Q&A provides the outline for the rest of the catechism:

2. Q. **What must you know to live and die in the joy of this comfort?**

   A. Three things:

   first, how great my **sin and misery** are;
   second, how I am **set free** from all my sins and misery;
   third, how I am **to thank God** for such deliverance.

(Romans 3:9-10; Matthew 5:16; Romans 6:13; Ephesians 5:8-10)

PART I: MISERY (Q&A 3-11)

"Part I: Misery" boldly names human sin and continuing disobedience of God's law as the reason we are alienated from God. Even though God "created [us] good and in his own image," Adam and Eve's "disobedience has so poisoned our nature that we are born sinners—corrupt from conception on. This is called "original sin." Because of it we cannot on our own keep God's law to love God, our neighbours, and ourselves (Matthew 22:37-39). In fact, "unless we are born again, by the Spirit of God," "we are so corrupt that we are totally unable to do any good." This is really bad news, but the Catechism tells us the good news next.

(Romans 3:9-20, 23; Genesis 1:26-27; Romans 5:12, 18-19)

PART II: DELIVERANCE (Q&A 12-85)

In "Part II:"Deliverance" (Q&A 12-85), the Catechism introduces us to the Lord Jesus Christ. Christ is "truly human and truly righteous," and "also true God." Therefore he can keep God's law perfectly. Jesus Christ is God's Son, the "mediator," who stands between God and humanity, "to set us completely free and to make us right with God."

Although we cannot save ourselves, with "true faith . . . created in [us] by the Holy Spirit through the gospel that everything God reveals in his Word is true [and] out of sheer grace earned for us by Christ, [our] sins [are] forgiven," and we are "made forever right with God, and have been granted salvation" (Q&A 21).

From Q&A 22-58 the Catechism teaches the Apostles' Creed phrase by phrase, since this is a summary of the Christian faith, "a creed beyond doubt, and confessed throughout the world." It is good for Christians to memorize this ancient confession. Notice that it is organized to introduce us to the blessed mystery of the Trinity, one God in three persons: Father and Creator; Jesus Christ, God's Son and our Savior; and the Holy Spirit who enables to do good once again.

THE APOSTLES' CREED

I believe in God, the Father almighty,
creator of heaven and earth.

I believe in Jesus Christ, his only Son, our Lord,
who was conceived by the Holy Spirit
and born of the virgin Mary.
He suffered under Pontius Pilate,
was crucified, died, and was buried;
he descended to hell.
The third day he rose again from the dead.
He ascended to heaven
and is seated at the right hand of God the Father
almighty.
From there he will come to judge the living and the
dead.

I believe in the Holy Spirit,
the holy catholic church,
the communion of saints,
the forgiveness of sins,
the resurrection of the body,
and the life everlasting. Amen.

THE TRINITY

Here are key questions and answers that follow the Apostles'
Creed and introduce us to the Trinity—God in three persons.

God the Father

26 Q.   What do you believe when you say,
        "I believe in God, the Father almighty,
        creator of heaven and earth"?
  A.   That the eternal Father of our Lord Jesus Christ
            who out of nothing created heaven and earth
            and everything in them,
            who still upholds and rules them
            by his eternal counsel and providence,
        is my God and Father
            because of Christ his Son.

(Genesis 1-2; Psalm 104)

28 Q.   How does the knowledge
        of God's creation and providence
        help us?
  A.   We can be patient when things go against us,
            thankful when things go well,
            and for the future we can have
            good confidence in our faithful God and Father
            that nothing will separate us from his love.
(Job 1:6-22; Romans 5:3-5; 8:38-39)

Jesus Christ—God the Son

29 Q. Why is the Son of God called "Jesus,"
meaning "savior"?

A. Because he saves us from our sins.
Salvation cannot be found in anyone else.

(Matthew 1.21, Acts 4.11-12)

31 Q. Why is he called "Christ,"
meaning "anointed"?

A. Because he has been ordained by God the Father
and has been anointed with the Holy Spirit
to be
our chief prophet and teacher
who perfectly reveals to us
the secret counsel and will of God for our
deliverance;
our only high priest
who has set us free by the one sacrifice of his
body,
and who continually pleads our cause with
the Father;
and our eternal king
who governs us by his Word and Spirit,
and who guards us and keeps us
in the freedom he has won for us.

(Luke 3:21-22; 4:14-19; John 1:18; 15:15;
Matthew 28:18-20; Revelation 12:10-11)

32 Q. Why are you called a Christian?

A. Because by faith I am a member of Christ
and so I share in his anointing.

I am anointed
to confess his name,
to present myself to him as a living sacrifice of
thanks,
to strive . . . against sin and the devil in this life,
and afterward to reign with Christ
over all creation
for all eternity.

(1 Corinthians 12:12-27; Joel 2:28; Romans 10:9-10; 12:1-2;
1 Peter 2:5-10; Ephesians 6:11)

33 Q. Why is he called God's "only Son"
when we also are God's children?

A. Because Christ alone is the eternal, natural Son of God.
We, however, are adopted children of God—
adopted by grace through Christ.

(Romans 8:14-17)

35 Q. What does it mean that Jesus "was conceived by
the Holy Spirit and born of the virgin Mary"?

A. That the eternal Son of God,
who is and remains
true and eternal God,
took to himself,
through the working of the Holy Spirit,
from the flesh and blood of the virgin Mary
a truly human nature
so that he might become David's true descendant,
like us in every way
except for sin.

(John 1:1-3, 14; Colossians 1:15-17; Luke 1:35;
Matthew 1:18-23; Hebrews 2:17; 7:26-27)

37 Q. What do you understand
by the word "suffered"?

A. That during his whole life on earth,
but especially at the end,
Christ sustained
in body and soul
the anger of God against the sin of the whole
human race.

This he did in order that
by his suffering as the only atoning sacrifice,
he might set us free, body and soul,
from eternal condemnation,
and gain for us
God's grace, righteousness, and eternal life.
(Isaiah 53; Romans 3:24-26; 8:1-4; John 3:16)

39 Q. Is it significant
that he was "crucified"
instead of dying some other way?

A. Yes.
This death convinces me
that he shouldered the curse
which lay on me,
since death by crucifixion was accursed by God.
(Galatians 3:10-13)

41 Q. Why was he "buried"?

A. His burial testifies
that he really died.
(John 19:38-42)

God the Holy Spirit

53 Q. What do you believe
   concerning "the Holy Spirit"?

A. First, he, as well as the Father and the Son,**
      is eternal God.
   Second, he has been given to me personally,
         so that, by true faith,
         he makes me share in Christ and all his
            blessings,
         comforts me,
         and remains with me forever.
(Genesis 1:1-2; 2 Corinthians 1:21-22; John 14:16-17)

**The Greek word translated "comforter" or "counselor" in
John 14 is *para-kletos*, referring to the Holy Spirit. *Parakletos*
is made up of two words meaning "the one called alongside."
The old English word "Paraclete," used in the hymn "Creator
Spirit, by Whose Aid" is hardly known now. That is why
some kids make jokes about parakeets. But if you ever feel far
from God, remember that Christians always can benefit from
the presence and person of "the one called alongside" us.

54 Q. What do you believe
   concerning "the holy catholic church"?

A. I believe that the Son of God
      through his Spirit and Word,
      from the beginning of the world to its end,
   gathers, protects, and preserves for himself
      a community chosen for eternal life
         and united in true faith.
   And of this community I am and always will be
   a living member.
(John 10:14-16, 27-30; Matthew 16:18; Romans 8:28-30)

55 Q. **What do you understand by
"the communion of saints"?**

A. First, that believers one and all . . .
    share in Christ
    and in all his treasures and gifts.

    Second, that each member
    should consider it a duty
    to use these gifts
        readily and cheerfully
        for the service and enrichments
            of the other members.
(1 Corinthians 12:4-7, 12-13; 12:20-27; Romans 12:4-8)

56 Q. **What do you believe
concerning "the forgiveness of sins"?**

A. I believe that God,
        because of Christ's atonement,
    will never hold against me
        any of my sins,
        nor my sinful nature
        which I need to struggle against all my life.

    Rather, in his grace
        God grants me the righteousness of Christ
        to free me forever from judgment.
(Psalm 103:3-4, 10, 12; Romans 7:21-25; John 3:17-18)

58 Q. How does the . . . "life everlasting" comfort you?

A. Even as I already now
    experience in my heart
    the beginning of eternal joy,
so after this life I will have
    perfect blessedness such as
        no eye has seen,
        no ear has heard,
        no human heart has ever imagined:
a blessedness in which to praise God eternally.

(Romans 14:17; John 17:3)

59 Q. What good does it do you to believe all this?

A. In Christ I am right with God
    and heir to life everlasting.

60 Q. How are you right with God?

A. Only by true faith in Jesus Christ.
    Even though my conscience accuses me
        of having grievously sinned against all God's
            commandments
        and of never having kept any of them
    and even though I am still inclined toward all evil,
    nevertheless,
        without my deserving it at all,
        out of sheer grace,
    God grants and credits to me
    the perfect satisfaction, righteousness, and holiness
        of Christ,
        as if I had never sinned or been a sinner,
        as if I had been as perfectly obedient
            as Christ was obedient for me.

61 Q. Why do you say that
by faith alone
you are right with God?

A. It is not because of any value my faith has
that God is pleased with me.
Only Christ's satisfaction, righteousness, and holiness
make me right with God.
And I can receive this righteousness . . .
by faith alone.

(Romans 10:10)

THE SACRAMENTS

66 Q. What are sacraments?

   A. Sacraments are holy signs and seals for us to see.
They were instituted by God so that . . .
he might make us understand more clearly
    the promise of the gospel. . . .

This is God's gospel promise:
to forgive our sins and give us eternal life
    by grace alone
    because of Christ's one sacrifice
    finished on the cross.

(Matthew 26:27-28)

68 Q. How many sacraments
    did Christ institute in the New Testament?

   A. Two: baptism and the Lord's Supper.

(Matthew 28:19-20; 1 Corinthians 11:23-26)

Baptism

69 Q.   **How does baptism**
        remind you and assure you
        that Christ's one sacrifice on the cross
        is for you personally?

A.   In this way:
        Christ instituted this [symbolic] outward washing
        and with it gave the promise that,
> as surely as water washes away the dirt from
>   the body,
> so certainly his blood and his Spirit
> wash away my soul's impurity,
>   in other words, all my sins.

(Acts 2:38; Romans 6:3-10)

74 Q.   **Should infants, too, be baptized?**

A.   Yes. Infants as well as adults
            are in God's covenant and are his people.
        They, no less than adults, are promised
            the forgiveness of sin through Christ's blood
            and the Holy Spirit who produces faith.

        Therefore, by baptism, the mark of the covenant,
            infants should be received into the Christian
                Church. . . .

        This was done in the Old Testament by circumcision,
            which was replaced in the New Testament by
            baptism.

(Genesis 17:7; 9-14; Colossians 2:11-13)

The Lord's Supper

75 Q. How does the Lord's Supper
remind and assure you
that you share
in Christ's one sacrifice on the cross
and in all his gifts?

A. Christ has commanded me and all believers
to eat this broken bread and to drink this cup.
With this command he gave this promise:

First,
as surely as I see . . .
the bread of the Lord broken for me
and the cup given to me,
so surely
his body was offered and broken for me
and his blood poured out for me
on the cross.
Second,
as surely as
I receive from the hand of the one who serves,
and taste with my mouth
the bread and cup of the Lord...
so surely
he nourishes and refreshes my soul
for eternal life
with his crucified body and poured-out blood.
(1 Corinthians 11:23-25)

76 Q. What does it mean
to eat the crucified body of Christ
and to drink his poured-out blood?

A. It means
to accept with a believing heart
the entire suffering and death of Christ
and by believing
to receive forgiveness of sins and eternal life.

But it means more.
Through the Holy Spirit, who lives both in
Christ and in us,
we are united more and more to Christ's
blessed body.
(John 6:35, 40, 50-58; 1 Corinthians 12:13;
Ephesians 4:15-16)

79 Q. Why does Christ call
the bread his body
and the cup his blood,
or the new covenant in his blood?

A. He wants to teach us that
as bread and wine nourish our temporal life,
so too his crucified body and poured-out blood
truly nourish our souls for eternal life.

But more important,
he wants to assure us, by this visible sign and pledge,
that we, through the Holy Spirit's work
share in his true body and blood
just as our mouths
receive these holy signs in his remembrance,
and that all of his suffering and obedience

are as definitely ours
as if we personally
had suffered and paid for our sins.
(1 Corinthians 10:16-17; Romans 6:5-11)

81 Q.   Who are to come to the Lord's table?
   A.   Those who are displeased with themselves
           because of their sins,
        but who nevertheless trust
           that their sins are pardoned
           and their continuing weakness is covered
               by the suffering and death of Christ,
        and who also desire more and more
           to strengthen their faith
           and to lead a better life.
(1 Corinthians 10:19-22; 11:26-32)

PART III: GRATITUDE (Q&A 86-129)

In "Part III: Gratitude" the Catechism uses the Ten Commandments (from the Old Testament) and the Lord's Prayer (from the New Testament) to explain how Christians can thank God on earth by doing good in daily life.

91 Q.   What do we do that is good?
   A.   Only that which
               arises out of true faith,
               conforms to God's law,
               and is done for his glory.
(Ephesians 2:10)

The Ten Commandments

92 Q.   **What does the Lord say in his law?**

  A.   God spoke all these words:
The First Commandment
I am the LORD your God,
    who brought you out of Egypt,
    out of the land of slavery.
You shall have no other gods before me.

The Second Commandment
You shall not make for yourself an idol
    in the form of anything in heaven above
    or on the earth beneath
    or in the waters below.
You shall not bow down to them or worship them;
    for I, the LORD your God, am a jealous God,
    punishing the children for the sin of the fathers
      to the third and fourth generation
      of those who hate me,
    but showing love to a thousand generations
      of those
      who love me and keep my commandments.

The Third Commandment
You shall not misuse the name of the LORD your God,
    for the LORD will not hold anyone guiltless
    who misuses his name.

The Fourth Commandment
Remember the Sabbath day by keeping it holy.
Six days you shall labor and do all your work,
but the seventh day is a Sabbath to the
    LORD your God.

On it you shall not do any work,
    neither you, nor your son or daughter,
    nor your manservant or maidservant,
    nor your animals,
    nor the alien within your gates.
For in six days the Lord made
    the heavens and the earth, the sea,
    and all that is in them,
but he rested on the seventh day.
Therefore the Lord blessed the Sabbath day
and made it holy.

The Fifth Commandment
Honor your father and your mother
    so that you may live long
    in the land the Lord your God is giving you.

The Sixth Commandment
You shall not murder.

The Seventh Commandment
You shall not commit adultery.

The Eighth Commandment
You shall not steal.

The Ninth Commandment
You shall not give false testimony
    against your neighbor.

The Tenth Commandment
You shall not covet your neighbor's house.
You shall not covet your neighbor's wife
   or his manservant or maidservant,
   his ox or donkey**,
   or anything that belongs to your neighbour.
(Exodus 20:1-17)

**Double penalty* for coveting talking donkeys like Balaam's
(Numbers 22; see p.162).

The Lord's Prayer

118 Q. **What did God command us to pray for?**
  A. Everything we need, spiritually and physically,
     as embraced in the prayer
     Christ our Lord himself taught us.

119 Q. **What is this prayer?**
  A. Our Father in heaven,
     hallowed be your name,
     your kingdom come,
     your will be done
       on earth as it is in heaven.
     Give us today our daily bread.
     Forgive us our debts,
       as we also have forgiven our debtors.
     And lead us not into temptation,
       but deliver us from the evil one.
     For yours is the kingdom
       and the power
       and the glory forever.
     Amen.
(Matthew 6:9-13)

NOTES & STUFF

NOTES & STUFF

NOTES & STUFF